PANIC To POWER

Strategies to Conquer Stress, Outsmart Overthinking and leap into action

NIDHI NAIR

HAPPINESS & SUCCESS COACH

In loving memory of my dearest mother, whose warmth and
wisdom will forever illuminate the pages of my life and
this book.

Contents

Contents

Procrastination

Acknowledgement

To my cherished daughter, Kyna Nair,

As I sit to pen down this acknowledgement, a multitude of emotions surge through me. This book, now a tangible reality, was once just a flicker of an idea, a whisper in my mind. It's a journey that has been as challenging as it has been rewarding, and through it all, you, my dear daughter, have been my unwavering pillar of strength and inspiration.

Your role in this journey has been far more profound than words can fully express. In the countless hours I spent wrestling with ideas and phrases, your presence was a calming force. You brought laughter into moments of frustration, clarity in times of confusion, and comfort during periods of doubt. Your unyielding faith in my abilities, even when I faltered, was a powerful motivator, urging me to press forward even when the path seemed daunting.

Your insights, sharp and perceptive, have been nothing short of a beacon of light guiding me through the creative fog. You have a special skill for sorting through many thoughts and ideas to find what's really important. Each feedback session with you was not just a discussion about the work at hand but a learning experience in itself. You taught me to look at my work from new perspectives, challenged me to push beyond my comfort zone, and inspired me to weave depth and sincerity into my writing.

Beyond your role as my most trusted critic and adviser, you have been a constant source of joy and love in my life. Your infectious enthusiasm for life, your unbridled passion for the little joys, and your profound empathy for the world around us have often been the spark that reignited my creative flame. In you, I see not just the child I raised but a remarkable individual who continues to teach me about life in ways I never imagined.

Your belief in this project was unwavering, even in moments when my own belief wavered. You saw the potential in my words even when they were just rough sketches of the ideas they eventually became. This book, in many ways, is a reflection of you – of the lessons you have taught me, of the strength you have shown me, and of the love that you have bestowed upon me.

As these pages go out into the world, they carry a piece of you with them – your spirit, your wisdom, and your love. I am immensely grateful for everything you have done and continue to do. Your presence in my life is a blessing I cherish every day.

Thank you, my dearest daughter, for being the heartbeat of this book and

"The light of my life"

I am filled with profound gratitude for all the mentors who have illuminated my path. To each of you, this acknowledgement is a small token of my immense appreciation.

To my early guides, who planted the seeds of curiosity and resilience in me, your wisdom has been the foundation upon which I built my dreams. Your encouragement during those formative years shaped not just the writer in me but the person I have become.

Thank you for sharing your knowledge, your time, and, most importantly, your belief in me. This book is not just a product of my efforts but a testament to the powerful impact of mentorship. I am eternally grateful.

Your belief in my abilities has been a constant source of strength and motivation.

Introduction

"It's up to you today to start making healthy choices. Not choices that are just healthy for your body, but healthy for your mind."

– Steve Maraboli

Have you ever realised life is so amazing at the same time? It's tricky when you think everything is going as per your plan. It gives you a surprise, good or bad, that is decided by your mental state and the situation. My journey of becoming a coach and helping thousands of people also started like this.

Change in life starts when we're either inspired or desperate; that's when we truly find the push to transform.

My life was a portrait of happiness—a devoted wife and mother. I was happy and content being a housewife taking care of my daughter and husband. Our life was not less than any dream as my husband was earning well, and we had more than all the things we needed in life. In the wheel of life, for me, family has always been 10/10. For my husband, Career, Finance, Fun, and Family were important. Their career and finances were going great as he was the head of South East Asia in an MNC and earning well. He used to give us his evenings and weekends without any interruptions (he was totally a family man), and for Fun, we used to travel a lot in India or Internationally.

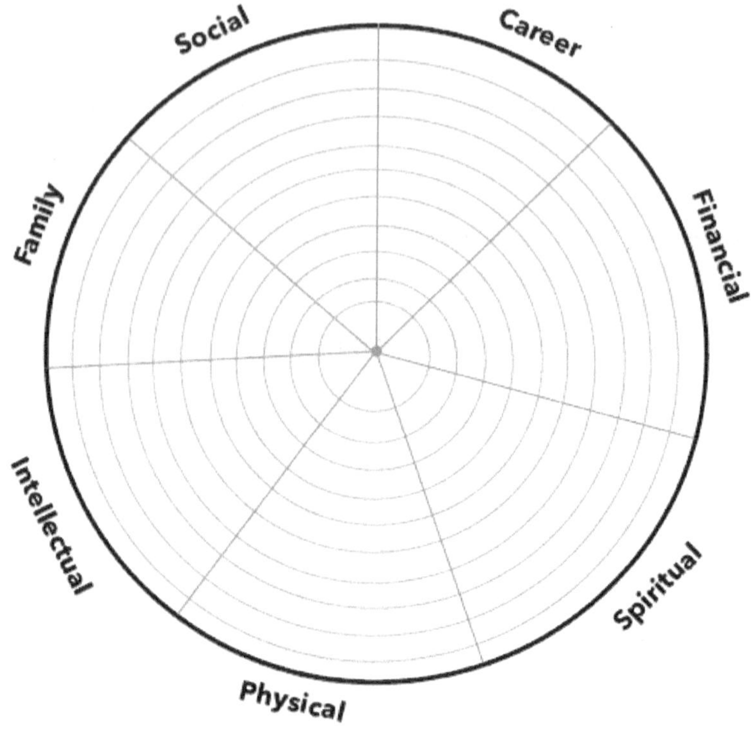

Image 1: Wheel of Life

But every good story has a villain; we, too, had one. In 2018, he lost his job things. One day, he came back from his office and told me that he had lost his job. I did not believe it because my husband is a funny guy and has done a lot of pranks on my daughter and me, so I thought this was one of his pranks. I told him not to talk nonsense and to be serious; he was dead serious. It was difficult for some time to digest, but I regrouped myself and told him it was okay to take it as a small vacation for all the hard work you have done in the last 17 years. He got a job in a few months and a good one; however, I started seeing changes in him. I started seeing he was unnecessarily thinking too much, taking stress, and procrastinating a lot of things because he was constantly comparing himself to his last job. He was internally fighting with himself; he started going into a shell, and I could see that very clearly. I could see that he was slowly getting into depression; there were no fun talks, no pranks, and very little family time.

Now, I clearly knew that this was the time he needed me the most; I left everything and started to spend more time with him. Understanding his needs and also starting to study his patterns, why is he getting angry? Why is he getting upset? I also started helping him to make him realise that things are good. It's just his mind that is playing with him and not showing him the real picture. It was a lot of push and patience from my side, which helped him realise the reality; he slowly started becoming his old self. That was a bulb-on-the-moment for me; if such a jolly character can slip into depression and anger, that means a lot of people in the world could be in the same situation.

I started studying NLP, Emotional Intelligence and mastered it; I took a lot of courses from the world's best so that I could give my best to society. For the past five years, I have assisted CEOs, managers, salespeople, accountants, counsellors, students, and parents. Meeting all of them, I have realised a few things. In the rush of our daily lives, we often find ourselves caught in a storm of stress, overthinking, and putting things off for later. It's like we're on a treadmill, running fast but staying in the same place. This book is your invitation to step off that treadmill and take a deep breath. The World Health Organisation has called stress the "Health Epidemic of the 21st Century," indicating its widespread effect on individuals' health, productivity, and well-being. I wrote this book for one reason: to be a wake-up call that will challenge those who are committed to living and being more to tap their God-given power.

We all know the feeling of being overwhelmed, of our minds racing with thoughts, and how easy it is to say, "I'll do it tomorrow." But here's the thing: these habits aren't just small roadblocks; they're signs that we're out of sync with our inner selves. They prevent us from living fully and experiencing the joy and peace that are our birthrights.

This book is about understanding why we fall into these patterns and, more importantly, how we can break free from them. It's not about complicated theories but simple truths and practices that can help us reconnect with who we truly are. We'll explore how stress, overthinking, and procrastination are more than just nuisances; they're signals calling us to pay attention to our inner world. And the beautiful part? The solutions are within us. Through mindfulness, self-awareness, and a few practical steps, we can find our way back to inner peace and alignment.

Join me on this journey. Together, we'll learn how to calm the storm inside, clear the clutter of our minds, and move forward with purpose and clarity. It's time to live the life you're meant to live, filled with peace, purpose, and joy. Let's start this beautiful journey together.

Stress

"Stress is like too much salt in our life's soup. Just the right amount can spice things up, but too much ruins the whole pot. It sneaks in when we're busy with work, family, or school, making us worried, tired, and grumpy. It's like carrying a backpack that gets heavier each day. But remember, every backpack has a zipper! Learning to deal with stress means finding that zipper — maybe it's a laugh with friends, a walk in the park, or a good book — so we can lighten the load and enjoy the soup of life!"

Harmony in Chaos

Out of clutter, find simplicity. From discord, find harmony. In the middle of difficulty lies opportunity.

– Albert Einstein

In the beautiful, complex journey of life, stress is a universal experience that connects us all, transcending borders and cultures. In my coaching career, I've seen how stress has woven itself into the fabric of our daily lives. It's important to recognise that the landscape of our experiences is always evolving, painting a dynamic picture of our collective journey.

This shared thread of stress, while challenging, also presents a powerful opportunity for growth and connection. It's a reminder that, despite our diverse backgrounds, we face common challenges that call for compassion, understanding, and collective action. In facing these challenges, we discover our shared humanity and the strength that comes from our interconnectedness.

The scenarios of stress around the world highlight the need for resilience and innovation. They urge us to look beyond our individual struggles and to come together in support of one another. As we navigate these waters, we're reminded of the incredible potential within each of us to adapt, overcome, and thrive.

Let this understanding serve as a catalyst for transformation. By embracing our shared experiences of stress as opportunities for learning and growth, we can pave the way for a more empathetic, supportive, and united world. Let us lead with our hearts, foster resilience within our communities, and work together to create a future where the bond of our common experiences becomes the foundation for collective well-being and prosperity.

As we move forward, remember that our ability to adapt and grow in the face of stress is a testament to the strong human spirit. Together, we can transform our challenges into stepping stones for a brighter, more connected world. The journey ahead is filled with possibility, and it's ours to shape with intention, courage, and an unwavering belief in our shared future.

Once, in a bustling city, there lived a woman named Lilly. Lilly was a picture of success by any standard. She was a high-flying executive at a major corporation, her calendar packed with meetings and business trips. Yet, beneath the surface of this seemingly perfect existence, Lilly was a vessel of stress and chaos.

Lilly's days were a whirlwind of activity. Her mornings began in a rush, often missing breakfast to beat the traffic. At work, her hours were filled with back-to-back meetings, endless phone calls, and a never-decreasing pile of emails. She often worked late, bringing her work home and eating into the time that should have been spent with her family or for herself. The rare free moments she found were spent worrying about the next day.

One evening, as Lilly sat alone in her office long after everyone had left, she felt a profound sense of emptiness. The city lights twinkled like distant stars, but their beauty failed to touch her. It was in this moment of solitude and silence that Lilly had an epiphany. She realised that in her pursuit of success, she had welcomed chaos into her life but had not learned to live with it harmoniously.

Determined to change, Lilly embarked on a journey of self-discovery. She realised that chaos would always be a part of her life, but she had the power to find harmony within it. She started practicing mindfulness, taking a few minutes each morning to meditate and prepare for the day. This simple act brought a sense of calm and focus that she had never experienced before.

Lilly also began to prioritise. She learned to say 'no' to unnecessary meetings and delegated tasks that didn't require her direct involvement. She discovered that not every email needed an instant reply. These small changes had a profound impact. Her work became more efficient, and for the first time in years, she left the office while the sun was still shining.

But the most significant change was in her mindset. Lilly stopped viewing chaos as her enemy. Instead, she saw it as a dynamic energy that, if harnessed correctly, could lead to creativity and growth. She began to approach problems with a calm, centred mindset, transforming challenges into opportunities.

As harmony replaced the chaos in her life, those around Lilly noticed the change. She became a source of strength and inspiration, leading her team not just with her mind but with her heart. Her relationships with her family blossomed, and she found joy in the small moments – a shared laugh, a quiet evening, a book read without haste.

Lilly's story is a testament to the fact that harmony is not the absence of chaos but the ability to find peace and purpose amidst it. It is a reminder that in the eye of the storm lies the calm, and in the heart of chaos, there lies the opportunity to create a symphony of harmony.

Exercise: The 5-Step Harmony in Chaos Transformation

Objective:

This exercise is designed to help you transform your relationship with chaos and stress, turning them into opportunities for growth, creativity, and harmony.

Duration:

One week (extendable as per individual preference).

1. Identify the Chaos:

- Task: Begin by identifying a specific area of chaos in your life. It could be work-related, personal, or even a broader existential concern.

- Reflection: Write down how this chaos makes you feel. Acknowledge these emotions without judgement.

2. Reframe Your Perception:

- Task: Take the identified chaos and actively reframe it. Instead of seeing it as a negative force, ask yourself, "What opportunity does this chaos present?"

- Reflection: Write down at least one positive perspective or opportunity that this chaos might be hiding.

3. Create an Action Plan:

- Task: Develop a small, actionable plan to tackle this chaos. Focus on steps that are within your control.

- Reflection: The plan should include specific actions, deadlines, and how these actions will help in transforming the chaotic situation.

4. Mindfulness and Visualisation:

- Task: Each morning, spend 5-10 minutes practicing mindfulness. Visualise yourself handling the chaotic situation successfully and with calmness.

- Reflection: After the visualisation, jot down any new feelings or thoughts that arise.

5. Review and Reflect:

- Task: At the end of the week, review your progress. Reflect on how your perception of the chaotic situation has changed and what impact your actions had.

- Reflection: Write down any changes in your stress levels, your thoughts about the chaos, and any other insights you gained.

Remember, chaos is not a pit but a ladder. Each rung represents an opportunity for growth, learning, and finding inner harmony. This exercise is a step towards not just climbing this ladder but also appreciating the view it offers.

Global Resonance:

The COVID-19 pandemic has acted as a wake-up call, revealing the deep interconnectedness of our lives and the collective vulnerability we share. This unprecedented challenge has ushered in a wave of stress and uncertainty, touching every corner of our existence. From health concerns to financial instability, the pandemic has forced us to confront the fragility of our systems and the importance of resilience.

Yet, within this chaos lies a profound opportunity for growth and transformation. It's as if we've been thrust into an unexpected journey, one that demands we harness our inner strength and adaptability. As we navigate through these turbulent times, we're reminded of the power of the human spirit and the importance of community. This moment in history is not just a test of our individual resolve but a call to unite, support each other, and emerge stronger.

In this shared experience, we find a mirror reflecting our collective fears and hopes. It's a reminder that our actions ripple across the globe, affecting lives far beyond our immediate view.

The pandemic challenges us to rethink our priorities, to value health and well-being above all, and to recommit to the well-being of our planet and its people.

As we move forward, let us embrace this journey with courage, open-heartedness, and a steadfast belief in our capacity to overcome. Let us transform this crisis into a catalyst for renewal, fostering a more compassionate, resilient, and interconnected world. The path ahead is ours to shape, guided by the lessons we've learned and the future we envision together.

Even when things seem chaotic, we can learn a lot about being strong and finding the good side of tough situations. These challenges are chances for us to show what we're really made of, to stay strong, and to handle whatever comes our way with a positive attitude. They teach us to be flexible, to care for others, and to stick together when things get hard.

Facing these big issues, how we react makes all the difference. We can choose to look for ways to make things better, to stay calm inside even when things outside are crazy, and to be kind and understanding with others. This is how we can change the stress around us into something positive.

Right now, the world needs leaders, and that means all of us. It's a time to use what we're going through as a chance to grow and to lead with a caring heart and a strong belief that we can make the future better. We're being called not just to get through tough times but to help create a better world filled with peace, success, and unity.

Together, we can change our stressful world into a place full of hope and opportunity. We have the power to shape the future, using what we've learned and our hopes for a better, united world.

CHAPTER 2

The Power of Presence

*"90% of what you're stressing about right now
won't even matter a year from now. Take a deep breath."*

– Mel Robbins

In our busy world, stress is a common problem that affects many people everywhere. But there's a way to deal with it: by focusing on the present moment. This idea is like finding a calm spot in the middle of a storm.

Let's look at the facts: a lot of people around the world are feeling stressed. It can make us feel bad physically and emotionally, and it can hurt our relationships and how happy we are with life.

However, the secret to overcoming stress is not about changing what's happening around us but changing how we think inside our minds. Mindfulness and being present in the moment can help us do this. It means paying full attention to what's happening right now without judging it.

By practicing mindfulness, we start to see our stressful thoughts and feelings as temporary, not permanent, parts of our lives. This helps us handle stress better because we learn to watch these thoughts and feelings without getting caught up in them.

Changing our approach to stress doesn't have to be hard. It can start with small steps, like taking deep breaths, enjoying our food, or noticing the world around us as we walk. These little moments of being present can make a big difference in reducing our stress.

So, as we learn more about how many people are dealing with stress, let's keep an open and mindful attitude. Mindfulness shows us that even when life gets tough, there's always a way to find peace and happiness by staying focused on the present. This journey can lead us to a better life filled with more joy and less stress.

1. The Universal Dance of Stress:

In life, stress is always around, kind of like a dance partner that never leaves. The World Health Organisation has found that a huge number of people, about 450 million, are dealing with mental health issues. This shows that many of us go through tough times. But it's important to remember that who we really are deep inside isn't affected by these stressful thoughts and feelings.

Realising this can make a big difference. It means that even when things get tough, there's a part of us that remains calm and strong. This inner part of us doesn't get shaken up by what's happening on the outside.

Seeing stress in this new light can help us learn from it instead of fighting against it. It's about asking ourselves what stress is trying to tell us about our lives and how we think. This can help us become stronger and more understanding people.

Dealing with stress this way isn't just a personal thing; it's something we all can do. It involves simple practices like paying attention to the present moment, taking deep breaths, and thinking about our experiences. These practices don't make stress disappear, but they can change how we feel about it, giving us a sense of peace and control.

This journey also helps us see that everyone goes through stress and mental health challenges, which means we should be kind and supportive of each other. We can create places where people feel comfortable asking for help and talking about their feelings.

So, in the "dance" of life, stress can help us grow. It can lead us to find a quiet strength inside ourselves and live a life that's full of purpose and happiness. Remembering that there's a calm and unshakeable part of us can guide us through life's ups and downs.

2. The Cost of Disconnection:

Stress doesn't just make us feel bad; it also costs a lot of money. Businesses lose about $300 billion every year because stress makes people less productive. This big number shows us how important it is to pay attention to the present moment instead of always worrying about work or money.

Being wealthy or successful isn't just about having lots of money or things. Real wealth comes from feeling peaceful and happy inside. When we're too focused on work or making money, we can forget to enjoy life and take care of our minds.

This problem isn't just about one person; it affects everyone. It makes us less creative, less able to work well, and less happy. To fix this, we need to change how we think about success. It's not just about what we do or how much we make but about enjoying the little moments and being present in what we're doing right now.

Simple things like paying attention to our breath, being thankful for what we have, and enjoying the moment can make a big difference. These practices help us focus on what's happening right now and make our lives fuller and happier.

By focusing more on the present, we can not only help fix the problem of lost money due to stress but also make our lives better.

It leads to more creativity, better relationships, and a balance between work and personal life.

So, the real cost of not paying attention to the present is missing out on the joy of life. Remembering to live in the moment is one of the best ways to be truly rich and happy.

3. Health as Harmony:

Chronic stress is like a quiet enemy that slowly harms our happiness and health. But it also reminds us to look inside ourselves for peace. It's telling us to pay more attention to the present moment, where we can find a natural balance between our body, mind, and spirit. This balance is where we can heal and feel whole again.

Being in the present moment helps us move beyond the problems caused by feeling disconnected from ourselves. When we focus on the "now," stress loses its power over us. We can let go of our worries and enjoy being alive. This isn't about running away from our problems but finding a real connection to the peaceful part of ourselves.

To live in the moment, we need to practice being mindful. This means paying attention to what's happening right now without judging it. It's about noticing our thoughts and feelings as they come and go without getting too caught up in them. This helps us stop reacting automatically to everything, which can bring us peace even when things around us are chaotic.

Living this way also lets us enjoy life more. We start to see beauty in ordinary things and feel grateful for the little joys of everyday life. It connects us to others and the world in a deeper way.

Finding our way back to living in the present isn't always easy. It asks us to be okay with quiet, to face what's really going on inside us, and to be true to ourselves. But even though it might feel uncomfortable at first, this is where we find our strength. It's how we heal, grow, and live a life full of meaning and happiness.

So, while chronic stress challenges us, it also offers a chance to change for the better. It's a call to wake up to what's happening right now and find the healing and happiness that come from being fully in the present moment.

4. The Pandemic Wake-Up Call:

The pandemic has been a tough time for everyone, making us all more stressed. But it's also a chance for us to wake up and see how important it is to live in the moment. When we focus on the here and now, we stop being so afraid and start finding our true strength.

This crisis has made us look at what's important in life, like our health, the people we care about, and feeling at peace inside. It's telling us to let go of the things we don't really need and to appreciate the simple moments. By doing this, we discover resilience, which means being able to get through tough times and come out stronger.

We're all learning from this together. It's a time to practice being mindful, which means paying attention to our thoughts and feelings without judging them. This helps us understand ourselves better and make good choices, even when things are hard.

The pandemic is also making us think about what matters most in life and how we can help others and our planet. It's a reminder to live with purpose and care about the bigger picture.

In the end, the pandemic is a challenge, but it's also an opportunity. It's teaching us to value the present moment, where we can overcome fear and find our true resilience. As we move forward, let's remember these lessons and work towards a world that's more aware, kind, and connected.

So, while chronic stress challenges us, it also offers a chance to change for the better. It's a call to wake up to what's happening right now and find the healing and happiness that come from being fully in the present moment.

5. The Workplace Symphony:

Work stress is a chance for us to bring more focus and attention to our jobs. As Eckhart Tolle often says, 'Realise deeply that the present moment is all you have. When we pay more attention to what we're doing right now at work, we can change stress into something that helps us do better and come up with new ideas.

In our jobs, where there's always so much to do and high expectations, it's easy to worry about the future or regret things from the past. But, if we learn to focus on what's happening right now, we can have more control over our work and feel better about what we're doing.

Paying attention to the present moment helps us see stress differently. It becomes a sign that tells us where we need to make changes or improve. This can lead us to think differently about our work, choose goals that really matter to us, and make sure our actions match those goals.

Being present at work also helps us deal with challenges in a positive way. We start to see problems as chances to learn and get better. This makes it easier to work with others, communicate well, and lead in a way that cares about everyone's success.

We can start being more present at work by doing simple things like taking deep breaths, really focusing on one task at a time, listening carefully to people, and thinking before we react. These small changes can make work less stressful and more enjoyable, increase our creativity, and make us more productive.

By focusing on the present, we find a new way to handle work stress. It's not about avoiding stress but learning to deal with it better. This way, stress can help us grow, come up with better ideas, and achieve success together.

Let's imagine you're working on a big project at work with a tight deadline. You're feeling overwhelmed because there's so much to do, and you're worried about not finishing on time. Here's how focusing on the present moment can help you deal with this stress and turn it into something positive:

Before Using Presence:

- You're constantly checking the clock, feeling the pressure build with each passing minute.

- You're worrying about what will happen if you don't finish the project on time, imagining negative outcomes.

- You're trying to work on multiple tasks at once, leading to mistakes and decreasing the quality of your work.

- You're snapping at co-workers because you're stressed and not really listening to what they're saying.

Applying Presence:

1. Take a Deep Breath: Start by taking a few deep breaths to calm your mind. This simple act can help reduce immediate stress and clear your head.

2. Focus on One task at a Time: Instead of trying to do everything at once, choose one specific task to focus on. Give it your full attention. This could be as simple as organising your workspace or outlining the next section of your project.

3. Mindful Listening: When a co-worker comes to talk to you, instead of thinking about your stress or what you need to

say next, really listen to them. You might find they have a suggestion that could help you with your project.

4. Pause and Reflect: Before reacting to an email or a comment from a co-worker, take a moment to pause. Use this time to calm any immediate emotional reaction and think about a constructive response.

After Using Presence:

- You find that focusing on one task at a time makes you more efficient, and your work quality improves.

- By not dwelling on the deadline constantly, you feel less anxious and more capable of completing your work.

- Listening to your co-workers not only improves your relationships but also opens opportunities for collaboration that can help you finish the project faster.

- Taking a moment to pause before reacting helps maintain a positive and productive work environment.

The Positive Outcome:

By applying presence to your work-life, you transform stress from being a source of anxiety and overwhelm into a catalyst for focused action and improved productivity. You learn to navigate workplace challenges with a clear mind and a calm approach, which not only benefits your work but also your overall well-being and relationships with co-workers.

6. Gender and Being:

In the complex world of gender roles, men and women often feel stress in different ways because of the different expectations placed on them. However, when we focus on living in the moment, everyone—no matter their gender—can find a peaceful place inside themselves. Stress then becomes a reminder for all of us to connect with something deeper than gender, a place of calm that we all share.

This idea tells us to look past the roles and labels society gives us and to find who we really are inside, where being male or female doesn't shape our peace of mind. Stress can help point us back to our true selves.

Women, who might be balancing work, family, and what society expects of them, can see stress as a signal to take time for themselves, to practice self-care, and to find moments of quiet despite their busy lives.

Men, who are often taught to hide their feelings and keep going no matter what can learn that acknowledging stress is okay. It can lead them to understand the importance of being kind to themselves and opening up about their feelings, which is a strength, not a weakness.

By being present in the moment, both men and women can handle stress better. This means doing simple things like taking deep breaths, paying full attention to what we're doing, really listening to others, and watching our thoughts and feelings without harsh judgement. These steps help us stay in the now, where stress lessens, and we see things more clearly.

Living in the moment gives us the power to choose how we react to tough situations. We realise that we might not be able to control everything that happens to us, but we can control how we respond. This understanding brings us peace and a feeling of control.

Also, as we make peace within ourselves, we help create a world that understands and cares more. Moving beyond gender stereotypes in how we deal with stress leads to stronger connections and a society that welcomes everyone. It shows that, deep down, we all want the same things: peace, happiness, and to feel connected.

So, when we deal with stress, it's not just a challenge; it's a chance to change. It invites everyone, no matter their gender, to find their inner peace and to help build a kinder, more inclusive world. This starts with the simple act of living in the present moment.

CHAPTER 3

Stress Unveiled: A Deeper Dive

Stress is a physiological and psychological response to a perceived threat or challenge. Stress is our body and mind's way of reacting to tough situations or changes. It's like an alarm that goes off inside us when we need to deal with something challenging. Everyone experiences stress, and it shows up in different ways, affecting our thoughts, feelings, and even our health.

On the one hand, stress can actually be good for us. It pushes us to try harder, learn new things, and overcome obstacles. It's a chance to grow and get stronger. But, if stress sticks around for too long without a break, it can start causing problems. It might make us feel tired all the time, give us headaches, or make us get sick more often. Mentally, it can make us feel worried, sad, or unable to think clearly.

So, dealing with stress isn't about getting rid of it completely—that's not possible since stress is a part of life. Instead, it's about learning how to handle it better. This means noticing when we're feeling stressed, understanding why, and using tools to help manage it. Things like taking time to relax, practicing mindfulness or meditation, staying active, and talking to friends or family can really help.

Thinking of stress as something we can learn from can also change how we see it. It can be a signal to look at our lives and see if we need to change something, whether it's how we think, what we value, or how we do things. When we see stress as a chance to grow, it can lead to positive changes.

Learning to manage stress is really about choosing how we react to challenges. This choice gives us the power to stay calm and keep going, even when things are tough. By getting better at dealing with stress, we not only feel happier and healthier ourselves but can also inspire others to do the same.

So, while stress can be tough, it also gives us a chance to learn about ourselves, become more resilient, and live life more fully. Facing stress in a positive way can lead to personal growth, happiness, and a deep sense of calm inside.

Major Types of Stress:

The two major types of stress are acute stress and chronic stress:

1. Acute Stress:

Acute stress is the most common and immediate form of stress. It arises in response to specific events or situations that require a rapid physiological and psychological response. Acute stress is the kind of stress we often run into when something needs our attention right now. It's like our body's alarm system for when we need to quickly deal with a problem or get away from something that might be dangerous. This "fight or flight" reaction can be exciting and give us a burst of energy, like when we're playing sports, performing on stage, going for exams, or rushing to meet a deadline. Once the situation is over, this stress usually goes away, and we feel normal again.

Even though it sounds intense, having acute stress occasionally isn't bad for us. It can teach us a lot about how to handle tough situations, make us stronger, and show us what we're capable of doing when we need to step up. It's all about how we look at these stressful moments and what we do with them.

But the trick is not to let this kind of stress get out of hand or happen too much. When we face acute stress, it's important to stay calm and focused. Techniques like taking deep breaths, being in the moment, and imagining positive outcomes can help us deal with it better. These methods help us stay grounded and make smart choices instead of panicking.

So, acute stress is just a part of life that can actually help us grow. By learning to manage it well, we can take on challenges with confidence and use them as opportunities to become better at dealing with whatever life throws our way.

Let's say you have a big presentation at work tomorrow. You've been preparing for weeks, but as the day approaches, you start to feel that familiar rush of nerves. This is acute stress in action. Your heart races, your palms get sweaty, and you might even feel a bit jittery. This is your body's way of getting you ready to face this challenge head-on, kicking your senses and focus into high gear.

Here's how you can manage this acute stress positively:

- **Acknowledge the Stress:** Recognise that feeling stressed before a big event is normal, and it's your body's way of preparing you to perform well.

- **Deep-Breathing:** Take a few moments to breathe deeply. Inhale slowly through your nose, hold for a few seconds, and then exhale slowly through your mouth. This helps calm your nervous system and clear your mind.

- **Visualise Success:** Close your eyes and imagine yourself giving the presentation confidently. Visualise the audience engaging positively, nodding, and smiling as you speak. This positive imagery can boost your confidence.

- **Prepare and Practice:** Go over your notes one last time and practice your speech. Knowing you're well-prepared can ease your stress.

- **Focus on the Present:** Instead of worrying about what might go wrong, focus on what you're doing right now. Whether it's going through your slides or practicing your speech, staying in the moment can keep stress at bay.

During the presentation, you might notice that acute stress actually helps you. You're more alert, your thoughts are clear, and you're able to think on your feet. Afterward, as you receive applause or positive feedback, you'll feel the stress melt away, replaced with a sense of accomplishment and relief.

2. Chronic Stress:

Chronic stress is a prolonged and persistent form of stress that persists over an extended period. Chronic stress is when stress doesn't stop, lasting for a long time because of ongoing problems like money worries, job issues, relationship troubles, or health concerns. Unlike stress, which comes and goes quickly, chronic stress hangs around and keeps our bodies in a constant state of alert. This can be bad for our health, leading to heart problems, a weaker immune system (making us get sick more easily), and mental health issues like anxiety and depression.

It's important to know the difference between short-term stress, which can be helpful for facing immediate challenges, and long-term chronic stress, which can harm our health if we don't deal with it. Managing chronic stress well can help us avoid these health problems.

To handle chronic stress, we can use different strategies. Practices like mindfulness and meditation can help calm our minds. Regular exercise can relieve physical tension and improve our mood. Having friends or family to talk to can make us feel supported and less alone. Sometimes, talking to a professional like a therapist can give us extra help and ways to cope.

Dealing with chronic stress is about more than just stopping the stress; it's about changing how we live to reduce stress in the first place. This means making choices that help us relax and feel better overall. By taking care of ourselves and managing stress, we can feel happier, healthier, and more ready to enjoy life.

Let's imagine a person who works a high-pressure job and is also dealing with long-term financial worries. They often feel tense, struggle to sleep, and find it hard to enjoy time with family or friends. This is chronic stress—it's not just about one bad day at work; it's about feeling this pressure day after day without a break.

Steps to manage stress:

1. Mindfulness Meditation: Every morning, before starting the day, spend 10 minutes practicing mindfulness meditation. Focusing on your breath and the present moment helps calm your mind and reduces feelings of anxiety.

2. Regular Exercise: Start going for a 30-minute walk every evening after dinner. This not only helps you unwind and clear your mind but also improves your sleep quality.

3. Talking About It: Open to a close friend about your financial worries and work stress. Just sharing your feelings makes you feel lighter and less alone. Your friend also offers some helpful advice and support.

4. Professional Help: Realising that your stress is affecting your quality of life, you decide to see a therapist. The therapist helps you develop strategies to manage your stress better and work through your financial worries.

5. Hobbies: Take up a hobby that brings you joy, such as gardening or painting on the weekends. This new activity gives you a sense of peace and accomplishment, helping you distract from your stress.

Over time, by applying these strategies, the person notices a significant improvement in their overall well-being. They feel more capable of handling the demands of their job and are less overwhelmed by their financial situation. Their relationships improve, and they start to enjoy their time again. This example shows how understanding and addressing chronic stress with positive actions can lead to a healthier, happier life.

Key Components of Stress:

1. Stressors:

These are the stimuli or events that trigger the stress response. Stressors can be external, such as work pressure, financial problems, or relationship issues, or internal, like self-imposed expectations or worries.

Stressors are things or situations that cause us to feel stressed. They can come from outside of us, like having too much work, money problems, or issues with friends or family. But stressors can also come from inside us, such as putting too much pressure on ourselves to be perfect or worrying too much about things that might happen in the future.

Understanding what causes our stress is important because it helps us figure out how to deal with it. For the stress that comes from outside, we might need to find better ways to handle our workload, get advice on managing our money, or talk things out with the people close to us. The goal is to manage these outside pressures in a way that doesn't make us feel overwhelmed.

For stress that comes from our own thoughts and feelings, it's about looking inside ourselves. This means learning to be kinder to ourselves, changing the way we think about things that stress us out, and accepting that it's okay not to be perfect.

Dealing with both outside and inside stressors means finding strategies that work for us. This could be practicing mindfulness, getting regular exercise, writing down our thoughts and feelings, or spending time with friends and doing things we enjoy. For the stress we create in our minds, we might try challenging our negative thoughts, using positive affirmations, or talking to a professional or therapist for help.

In short, stressors, whether they come from our environment or from within us, are a chance for us to grow and learn more about ourselves. By figuring out how to handle these stressors, we can make our lives better, not just getting by but thriving and making the most out of every day.

2. The Stress Response:

When the brain perceives a stressor, it activates the "fight or flight" response. When our brain notices something stressful, it starts the "fight or flight" response. This is our body's way of getting ready to either deal with the problem or run away from it. The brain does this by releasing stress hormones like cortisol and adrenaline. These hormones make our heartbeat faster, raise our blood pressure, and give us a burst of energy so we're ready to face the challenge.

This stress response is a sign of how strong and adaptable we are. It helps us do things like speak up during an important meeting, quickly steer away from an accident, or handle tough situations with others. It's our body's way of helping us be alert and do our best in tricky situations.

But it's also important to know how to calm down after the stressor is gone, especially today when most of our stress is about things like work or personal issues, not physical dangers. Learning how to relax and tell our body it's safe now is key. This can be done through practices like mindfulness (paying attention to the present moment), taking deep breaths, exercising, or spending time with friends and family. These activities help our body understand that the stressful situation is over and it's time to relax.

Seeing stress as something we can handle can change how we deal with tough situations. It encourages us to look at challenges as chances to grow and get better at dealing with stress. This way, we not only get through difficult times but also learn and grow from them.

So, the "fight or flight" response is a natural part of how we deal with stress. It shows we have what it takes to face challenges head-on. By managing this response well, we can handle life's ups and downs more smoothly and feel more confident and capable.

3. Physiological Changes:

The stress response leads to various physiological changes; when we're stressed, our body goes through a bunch of changes to get us ready to face a problem or run away from it. Our heart beats faster to pump blood to our muscles and important organs quickly. Our blood pressure goes up, helping our body get more oxygen and nutrients where they're needed. We also start breathing faster to take in more oxygen, and we become super alert, making us more aware of everything around us. This is all our body's way of preparing us to deal with whatever's causing the stress.

These changes are great for short moments when we need to act fast. But they're not meant to last a long time. After the stressful situation is over, our body needs to calm down and rest. This is why knowing how to relax after feeling stressed is important. It helps our body recover and stay healthy.

Understanding how our body reacts to stress shows us how strong and ready we can be when we need to deal with tough situations. But it also reminds us that taking care of ourselves by relaxing and taking it easy is just as important. This balance helps us handle stress better and keeps us feeling good in the long run.

4. Impact on Health:

Prolonged exposure to stress is associated with a range of health issues; when stress sticks around for too long, it can start causing real problems for our health. It's like carrying a heavy backpack all the time. Eventually, it's going to wear you down.

Here are some of the ways long-term stress can hurt us:

Heart Trouble: Too much stress can make it hard on our hearts, leading to high blood pressure and increasing the risk of heart problems like heart attacks.

Getting Sick More Often:

Our body's system for fighting off germs doesn't work as well when we're always stressed, so we might catch colds and other infections more easily.

Stomach Issues: Stress can mess with our stomachs and digestion, leading to stomach aches, heartburn, or even more serious issues like ulcers.

Feeling Anxious or Sad: Stress can also affect how we feel emotionally, making us more likely to feel nervous, anxious, or depressed.

Understanding the impact of stress is like having a roadmap to better health. It shows us that taking steps to reduce stress is important, not just for feeling better now but for staying healthy in the long run. With the right approach, we can handle life's challenges more easily and live a happier, healthier life.

5. Coping Mechanisms:

When it comes to dealing with stress, we all have different ways of handling it. Some of these methods are helpful and can make us stronger, while others might seem to make things easier at first but can cause more problems in the long run.

Helpful Strategies (Adaptive Coping): These are the good ways we deal with stress. They involve facing the problem directly or finding healthy ways to manage how we feel. For example, if we're stressed about a big project, breaking it down into smaller tasks and working on it bit by bit is a helpful strategy. Talking to friends or family about what's bothering us or doing activities like meditation and exercise are other great ways to handle stress. These methods help us feel better and grow stronger.

Not-So-Helpful Strategies (Maladaptive Coping): These methods might seem like they help because they make us feel better quickly, but they don't solve the problem and can make things worse. Using alcohol or drugs to forget about stress, ignoring the problem, or putting off tasks are examples of not-so-helpful ways to cope. While these might give us short-term relief, they can harm our health and make our stress even bigger in the long run.

Choosing to deal with stress in healthy ways isn't always easy, but it's worth it. It means facing our problems head-on and finding ways to manage our feelings that are good for us. This doesn't just help us get through tough times; it makes us better at handling whatever life throws at us in the future.

By using helpful strategies to cope with stress, we're taking steps towards building a happier and more fulfilling life. We're not just getting rid of stress for now; we're preparing ourselves to be stronger in facing future challenges.

6. Individual Variability:

In life, how we deal with stress is very personal. Our genes, personality, and what we've been through all play a part in how we handle tough situations. What might really stress one person out might not bother someone else as much.

It's also important to remember that not all stress is bad. Some stress, called "eustress," is good for us. It can motivate us and push us to reach our goals, like the excitement we feel when working on a project we're passionate about or facing a challenge we're eager to overcome.

However, if we're always stressed and don't find ways to deal with it, it can start to harm our health. This kind of long-term stress can make us feel down, both physically and mentally, and can lead to serious problems if we don't handle it well.

To manage stress, we need to first understand what's causing it. Then, we can find healthy ways to cope with it, like talking to friends, exercising, or practicing mindfulness. These strategies can help reduce the stress we feel.

Building resilience, or the ability to bounce back from tough times, is also important. It's about learning from challenges and keeping going, even when things get hard. This helps us not just get through stressful times but grow stronger because of them.

In short, healthily dealing with stress is about knowing ourselves, using positive strategies to cope, and building our strength to face life's challenges. This isn't just about fighting off stress; it's about learning how to live a happy and fulfilling life despite the challenges we face.

CHAPTER 4

Science Behind the Stress

The science behind stress involves complex interactions between the brain, nervous system, and various physiological processes. When an individual encounters a stressor, whether it's a physical threat or a psychological challenge, the body initiates a series of responses to cope with the perceived danger.

The biology of stress is like our body's alarm system. It gets us ready to face tough situations or to run away from them. Here's how it works, broken down into simple steps, with examples:

1. Noticing Stress:

Imagine you see a large animal running towards you, sounding loud. Your brain, specifically a part called the amygdala, notices this as a threat and tells another part of your brain, the hypothalamus, that there's danger.

2. Fight or Flight Response:

The hypothalamus acts like a command centre and tells your body to get ready to either fight the animal or run away as fast as you can. This is done by sending signals that make your adrenal glands release adrenaline, a hormone that makes your heart beat faster and gives you a burst of energy.

3. Cortisol Comes into Play:

Along with adrenaline, your body also releases cortisol, another stress hormone. This is like giving your body a big cup of coffee to use more sugar for energy and put on hold other things it might be doing, like digesting food, so you can focus on the dangerous animals around you.

4. Your Body's Reaction:

Your heart races and your blood pressure goes up so you can run faster or defend yourself.

- You breathe faster to take in more oxygen.
- You might feel your stomach turn because your body has stopped digestion to deal with the threat.

5. Calming Down:

Once the animal is gone, and you realise it's safe, your body's "rest and digest" system kicks in to calm everything down. Your heart rate goes back to normal, and your body stops pumping out so much adrenaline and cortisol.

But if you're always stressed—like if every day feels like you're facing that.

Big Animal—your body keeps pumping out cortisol. This can make you feel sick and tired or even lead to more serious health problems like heart disease or trouble sleeping.

So, managing stress is like teaching your body's alarm system to tell the difference between a real emergency (like an animal) and something that's not actually a threat (like worrying about a big project). Simple things like taking deep breaths, exercising, or talking to a friend can help turn off the alarm when it's not needed, keeping you healthier and happier.

CHAPTER 5

Stress Unveiled: Exploring Hidden Culprits – Causes of Stress

Stress can arise from various sources, and the causes of stress, known as stressors, can vary widely among individuals. Here are common categories of stressors:

1. Workplace Stress:

Workplace stress is like a heavy backpack we carry around because of too much work, tight deadlines, worrying about losing our jobs, not getting along with co-workers, and feeling like we have no control over our work-life. It's like being pushed closer to the edge of a cliff, with each problem adding more weight to the backpack.

This kind of stress isn't just uncomfortable; it can make us feel tired, anxious, and unable to enjoy life. Our bodies are always on high alert, making it hard to sleep and relax and leaving us feeling drained all the time.

However, facing workplace stress also gives us a chance to grow stronger and take control. It's about setting clear limits, asking for deadlines that make sense, talking things out with co-workers, and feeling more in control of our work.

High work demands, tight deadlines, job insecurity, conflicts with colleagues, and a lack of control over one's work environment can contribute to stress in the workplace.

2. Life Changes:

Big changes in life, like getting married, going through a divorce, moving to a new place, having a baby, or losing someone we love, can really shake things up. These events change our routine and bring new challenges, making us feel like we're stepping into unknown territory.

Even though these changes can be stressful, they also give us a chance to grow. It's like going on an adventure where we learn a lot about ourselves and become stronger. Whether it's the happiness of adding a new member to the family or the sadness of saying goodbye to someone, each of these moments teaches us something important.

To get through these times, it helps to stay flexible and lean on the things and people that matter most to us. It's also important to take care of ourselves by doing things that keep us calm and centred, like meditating, exercising, or spending time outside.

Every big change in life is an opportunity to see things in a new way and to make our lives even better. These moments might be tough, but they're also when we can make some of our most meaningful memories. So, as we face these changes, let's try to stay open and brave, knowing that each step forward is a chance to write a new, exciting chapter of our story.

3. Financial Stress:

Money problems, like being in debt, worrying about losing your job, or dealing with a shaky economy, are big reasons why many of us feel stressed. Trying to pay bills on time and wanting to keep up or improve our way of living can add to that stress.

Imagine you're walking close to the edge of a cliff, and each money worry is like a strong wind trying to push you off balance. Being in debt is like carrying a heavy backpack that makes every step harder. Not being sure if you'll have a job tomorrow is like trying to walk in fog—you can't see where you're going. And when the whole economy is unstable, it's like the ground is moving under your feet.

But facing money stress can also be a chance to get smarter about handling our finances. It's about learning to manage our money better by budgeting, saving, and understanding how to grow our money through investing. It means planning for our money that helps us feel secure and reach our dreams.

Getting through money stress also means asking for help when we need it—like getting advice from money experts or talking to friends and family. Sometimes, just knowing you're not alone can make a big difference.

Dealing with money stress also teaches us to be flexible. Sometimes, we might need to change how we live to match what we can afford, but that doesn't mean we can't be happy. Knowing what's important to us helps us enjoy life, no matter how much money we have.

So, while dealing with money issues is tough, it also helps us grow. It's not just about making it through tough times but about learning how to thrive, understanding our money better, and building a life that's rich in what truly matters.

4. Relationship Issues:

When we have problems with the people we're close to, like our partner, family, or friends, it can stress us out. This could be because we're not getting along, we're not talking properly, or we're just finding it hard to understand each other.

Think of each relationship as a thread in a big piece of fabric that makes up your life. When everything's going well, the fabric looks great and feels good. But when there are knots in the threads—like arguments or misunderstandings—the fabric doesn't look or feel so nice anymore.

But these tough times are chances for us to grow and make our relationships stronger. It means we must talk things out, even if it's uncomfortable, and listen to each other. It's about being honest and open and sometimes looking at how we might be part of the problem, too.

It's also important to try to understand how the other person is feeling. This can help break down walls and bring us closer together.

So, when we're going through hard times with people we care about, it's not just a problem to solve. It's a chance to understand each other better, to say sorry if we need to, and to work on making our relationship even stronger.

By facing these challenges bravely and with an open heart, we can turn stressful times into opportunities to build deeper connections with the people who matter most to us. This not only helps us feel better but also makes our relationships richer and more meaningful.

5. Health Concerns:

Chronic illnesses, injuries, or the diagnosis of a serious health condition can be immensely stressful. The uncertainty, lifestyle adjustments, and emotional impact of health issues contribute to stress.

When we face health problems like long-term sickness, getting hurt, or finding out we have a serious illness, it's tough. This isn't just about dealing with being sick or hurt; it's also about the worry, having to change how we live, and dealing with all the emotions that come with it.

Imagine you're sailing a boat, and suddenly, a big storm hits. Getting sick or injured is like that lightning strike that lights up the sky, showing us how fragile life can be. What comes next is a journey that can be hard: trying to figure out treatments, adjusting to new ways of doing things, and asking, "Why did this happen to me?"

But, even in these hard times, we can find a chance to grow and see life differently. We learn to figure out what's important, to not take things for granted, and to enjoy the simple things.

Dealing with the stress of health issues means doing a few things:

- Keeping a positive attitude and believing we can get through this.
- Asking for help and support from friends, family, or doctors.
- Taking good care of ourselves, following doctor's advice, and doing things that make us happy and relaxed.

In short, health problems test us, but they also give us a chance to learn a lot about ourselves. They teach us to cherish life, lean on our loved ones, and find strength we might not have known we had. By facing these challenges bravely and with hope, we can get through the tough times and maybe even come out stronger on the other side.

6. Environmental Factors:

Our surroundings, like where we live and the quality of our environment, play a big role in how stressed we feel. Things like constant loud noise, air pollution, or experiencing natural disasters like floods or earthquakes can make us feel really stressed. These situations can make us feel like we're facing big problems that we can't fix on our own.

But even when things seem tough because of our environment, we have the power to make changes. We can start by making our own spaces more peaceful and healthier. This might mean making our homes quieter and cleaner or finding little ways to bring nature and calm into our lives.

We can also work with others to help fix bigger environmental problems. This could be doing things to reduce pollution, helping in community clean-ups, or supporting laws that protect the environment. When we work together, we can make a big difference.

It's also important to try and see the good around us, even when things aren't perfect. This means noticing the beauty in nature and remembering that both nature and people are good at bouncing back after tough times.

So, dealing with stress from environmental problems isn't just about feeling better ourselves. It's also about coming together to take care of our planet. By doing this, we're not only reducing our stress but also helping make the world a better place for everyone.

7. Daily Hassles:

Everyday challenges are termed "daily hassles." Every day, we face small challenges, like getting stuck in traffic, having little disagreements, feeling rushed, or dealing with annoying things. On their own, these might not seem like a big deal, but when they happen a lot, they can make us feel stressed out over time.

Think of it like walking on a path where there are lots of small pebbles. One pebble might not bother you, but if your shoes start to fill up with them, walking becomes uncomfortable. This is what happens when everyday hassles keep adding up; they start to make our day harder and can even make us feel less happy.

But there's a silver lining here. Dealing with these small daily hassles can help us grow stronger. It's not about getting rid of all the hassles in our lives; it's about learning how to handle them better so they don't bother us as much. This means focusing on the good things in our lives, staying calm in the moment, and finding ways to deal with stress, like exercising or taking deep breaths.

We can also get better at saying "no" sometimes and deciding what's important to spend our time on. This helps us take control of our day and feel less overwhelmed.

So, even though these daily hassles can be annoying, they also give us a chance to learn how to stay calm and happy, no matter what comes our way. By looking at these small challenges as opportunities to improve, we can make our everyday lives smoother and more enjoyable.

8. Technology and Information Overload:

Constant connectivity, information overload, and the pressure to keep up with technology can be sources of stress. The fast-paced nature of the modern world can contribute to feeling overwhelmed.

In today's world, we're always connected to our phones and computers, getting non-stop messages, news, and all sorts of information from the internet. It's like trying to drink water from a fire hose—there's just too much, and it can make us feel stressed and overwhelmed.

But imagine if we could control that flow of information, choosing when to open the tap and when to close it. We can start by setting some rules for how we use technology, like turning off notifications for apps that aren't important or setting aside specific times to check emails and social media. It's like making a quiet space in our day where we can take a break from the noise of the internet.

We also need to be smart about how we use technology. This means learning about the gadgets and apps we use and figuring out ways to make them work for us, not against us. It's about using technology to make our lives better, not letting it control us.

By being more mindful about our use of technology, we can enjoy the benefits without feeling overwhelmed. We can focus on having more meaningful conversations online instead of trying to keep up with everything. This way, we can stay connected without losing our peace of mind.

So, dealing with the stress of technology and too much information is about making choices—choosing what to pay attention to, when to take a break, and how to use technology in a way that's good for us. This helps us take advantage of what the digital world offers without letting it overwhelm our lives.

9. Social and Cultural Expectations:

In society, there are a lot of rules about how we should act, what we should do, and even who we should be. These rules can include things like gender roles, what's considered "normal" behaviour, and other pressures from our culture. Trying to live up to these expectations can be stressful, especially if they don't match up with who we are or what we want.

Think of it like trying to balance on a tightrope where one side is what society expects of you, and the other side is your true self. It can be tricky not to fall off and stressful trying to stay balanced.

But facing these challenges is also a chance for us to grow stronger and make changes in society. It's about being true to ourselves, even if that means not following every rule or expectation that society sets for us.

To deal with this stress, it's important to really know and understand ourselves—what we believe in, what's important to us, and who we want to be. This helps us decide which societal expectations we want to follow and which ones we don't.

It's also important to surround ourselves with people who support us just the way we are. Having a community that accepts and celebrates our true selves can make it a lot easier to handle the stress of societal pressures.

In short, while society's rules can be stressful, they also give us a chance to stand up for our true selves and help make the world a more accepting place for everyone. By being true to ourselves and finding support from others, we can navigate these pressures and live a life that's true to who we are.

Societal and cultural expectations, including gender roles, societal norms, and cultural pressures, can contribute to stress as individuals navigate these expectations.

10. Self-Imposed Pressure:

Setting excessively high standards, perfectionism, and unrealistic expectations for oneself can lead to self-imposed stress. The constant drive for achievement may contribute to feelings of inadequacy.

When we try hard to be perfect and set super high standards for ourselves, we can end up causing ourselves a lot of stress. It's like we're always trying to reach the top of a mountain that keeps getting taller every time we get close. This can make us feel like we're never doing enough, even when we're doing a lot.

It's important to remember that stress affects everyone differently. What makes one person feel stressed might not bother someone else at all. And sometimes, it's not just one big thing that stresses us out, but a bunch of smaller things all adding up.

To handle the stress we put on ourselves, we need to start being a bit easier on ourselves. We need to understand that it's okay not to be perfect and to celebrate the small wins along the way. Setting goals that are achievable and not being too hard on ourselves when things don't go exactly as planned can help.

Finding ways to deal with stress, like taking time to relax, talking to friends, or practicing mindfulness, can make a big difference. These strategies can help us feel better and more in control, even when we're pushing ourselves to achieve our goals.

In short, it's great to aim high and try to do our best, but it's also important to be kind to ourselves. By setting realistic goals and recognising all the progress we're making, we can reduce the stress we feel and enjoy our journey a lot more...

CHAPTER 6

The Silent Messengers: Understanding Stress in the Body (Symptoms of Stress)

Stress can manifest in various ways, affecting both the mind and body. Here are common symptoms of stress:

1. Physical Symptoms:

Headaches or migraines.

Muscle tension and stiffness.

Fatigue and low energy.

Sleep disturbances (insomnia or oversleeping).

Changes in appetite or digestive issues.

Increased heart rate and palpitations.

Sweating or cold, clammy hands.

2. Emotional and Behavioural Symptoms:

Irritability or mood swings.

Anxiety or restlessness.

Depression or feelings of sadness.

Difficulty concentrating or making decisions.

Changes in appetite and eating habits.

Increased use of alcohol, tobacco, or other substances.

Social withdrawal or isolation.

3. Cognitive Symptoms:

Racing thoughts or constant worrying.

Forgetfulness and memory issues.

Difficulty concentrating or focusing.

Negative self-talk and self-doubt.

Poor judgement or decision-making.

Trouble organising thoughts and tasks.

4. Interpersonal Symptoms:

Increased conflicts or arguments with others.

Difficulty communicating effectively.

Withdrawal from social activities or relationships.

Impatience or irritability with others.

Decreased empathy or compassion.

5. Work and Academic Symptoms:

Decreased productivity and performance.

Procrastination or difficulty meeting deadlines.

Increased absenteeism or tardiness.

Difficulty making decisions at work or in academics.

Burnout or feelings of being overwhelmed.

6. Physical Health Symptoms:

A weakened immune system leads to frequent illnesses.

Chronic pain or tension in the body.

Gastrointestinal issues, such as stomachaches or irritable bowel syndrome (IBS).

Increased risk of cardiovascular problems.

Changes in sexual desire or performance.

7. Behavioural Changes:

Nervous habits, such as nail-biting or pacing.

Changes in sleep patterns, such as insomnia or oversleeping.

Increased use of substances like caffeine or comfort foods.

Impulsive behaviours or risk-taking activities.

Changes in personal hygiene and self-care habits.

It's important to note that individuals may experience a combination of these symptoms, and the severity of symptoms can vary. Additionally, chronic stress can contribute to the development or exacerbation of certain health conditions. Recognising these symptoms is crucial for proactive stress management, and seeking support from healthcare professionals or mental health experts may be beneficial for effective coping strategies.

Overthinking

"Everybody is a genius. But if you judge a fish by its ability to climb a tree, it will live its whole life believing that it is stupid."

– Albert Einstein

The Overthinking Dilemma

Introduction:

Overthinking refers to excessive and repetitive dwelling on thoughts, ideas, or situations, often beyond what is necessary or productive. It involves analysing and reanalysing information or events, sometimes to the point of creating a state of mental rumination. Overthinking can lead to heightened stress, anxiety, and mental exhaustion as individuals become trapped in a cycle of worry and indecision.

Overthinking is the silent productivity killer, my friends. Think this: you've got a brilliant mind, a powerhouse of potential, and a world of opportunities waiting for you. But then, there's this sneaky little saboteur called 'overthinking' that creeps in and starts wreaking havoc on your mental landscape.

Here's the deal: Your mind is an incredible tool designed to solve problems, create solutions, and propel you toward success. But when overthinking takes the reins, it's like putting a Ferrari in reverse. You've got all this horsepower, but you're not going anywhere!

Overthinking is essentially your mind working overtime, juggling thoughts and scenarios like a circus performer on a unicycle. It's natural to reflect and analyse, but when it turns into an endless loop of second-guessing, questioning, and worrying, that's when trouble brews.

Why does it matter? Well, my friends, it's all about efficiency. When you overthink, you're stealing precious mental bandwidth from what matters — making decisions, taking action, and moving forward. It's like having a supercomputer and using it to play tic-tac-toe instead of solving the world's problems.

Understanding Overthinking:

1. Impact on Productivity:

The impact of overthinking on productivity is akin to a silent thief stealing precious moments of focused work.

Think of overthinking like a sneaky thief stealing time from getting work done.

Meet Sarah, a project manager with tight deadlines. As she thinks about her project, doubts start popping up. She keeps going back to her decisions, and this doesn't just make her tired; it also slows down how much she can get done.

Sarah is ready to work, but overthinking is like a sneaky thief stealing her focus and energy. Instead of making progress, she is stuck thinking too much.

Now, here's the thing – this overthinking thief is not just stealing time; it's affecting Sarah's ability to do her job well. Her energy is getting drained, and she's not as productive as she could be.

But there's good news! To beat this sneaky thief, Sarah needs to focus on doing things instead of thinking too much. Break the project into smaller tasks, make decisions without second-guessing too much, and trust those decisions. This way, Sarah can take back control and make real progress.

In simple terms, overthinking is like a thief stealing time and energy. But Sarah has the power to stop this thief by focusing on doing the work instead of thinking too much. That's the key to getting things done and being successful.

2. Impact on Decision-Making:

In the realm of decision-making, overthinking casts a shadow that can obscure even the most straightforward choices.

Think of decision-making as a path to progress. Now, meet Michael, a boss facing a big decision for the business. Deciding should be like shooting arrows straight to the target, quick and precise. But there's this sneaky thing called overthinking that clouds the path.

Imagine Michael standing at a crossroads, thinking about the decision. The possibilities and the fear of making a wrong choice make his thoughts spin around and around. This overthinking doesn't just affect Michael; it slows down the whole team and the project timeline.

In the world of easy decision-making, "Decide fast and take action."

Overthinking is like a fog over the path – it makes decisions slow and uncertain.

Michael needs to break free from this loop. Instead of thinking about every little thing, he should focus on what really matters. What aligns with the goals? What are the important factors? Then, he can trust his gut and make that decision.

Remember, not making a decision is a decision to stay stuck. In the easy world, Michael learns to see the overthinking shadow, steps into the light of action, and ensures that decisions made move everyone forward. The lesson is simple: quick decisions keep progress rolling.

3. Impact on Overall Well-Being:

"Let's take a step back and look beyond the busy workplace into the lives of professionals. Imagine the echoes of overthinking reaching far beyond the office walls, creating ripples in the broader spectrum of their lives. This isn't just about work; it's about how the continuous mental chatter can spill over into personal relationships, affecting the ability to fully enjoy life outside the job.

Think of a professional, let's call her Sarah, who, after a long day at work, finds it hard to switch off that mental chatter. She's carrying the weight of decisions and thoughts into her personal life. It is an overthinking trap where the boundaries between work and personal life start to blur.

Now, Sarah, caught in the overthinking loop, is not just carrying her work on her shoulders; she's also carrying it into her personal moments. This blurring of boundaries becomes an extra burden on her already overwhelmed self.

Life is a series of roles – a professional at work, a friend in social circles, a family member at home. Overthinking, my friends, blurs these roles. It's like wearing your work hat when you should be wearing your personal hat and vice versa.

Here's the advice: Professionals need to set clear boundaries. When work is over, it's time to mentally close that office door. Instead of carrying the work baggage, focus on being present in personal moments. This means enjoying time with family, connecting with friends, and giving the mind a break.

Maintaining a healthy work-life balance isn't just a luxury; it's a necessity for long-term success and happiness. Overthinking might be a persistent visitor, but professionals need to show it the exit when the workday is done.

So, in the easy world, Sarah learns to draw clear lines between work and personal life, shedding the overthinking baggage when the office door closes. By doing so, she lightens her load, finds more joy in personal relationships, and ensures that the echoes of overthinking don't drown out the melody of a well-balanced life.

As we embark on this journey to understand and conquer the overthinking dilemma in the professional realm, we invite you to reflect on your own experiences. Have you, too, found yourself entangled in the intricate threads of overthinking? If so, fear not, for this book is a guide—an exploration into strategies and insights to untangle the knots, reclaim focus, and forge a path toward a more mindful and productive professional journey.

CHAPTER 2

Why We Overthink

Now, let's delve into the fascinating topic of why we overthink.

A puzzle that often baffles many of us: you've got thoughts swirling around in your head like leaves caught in a whirlwind, and it seems impossible to turn off the mental chatter.

The reasons behind overthinking with practical insight.

1. Fear of Failure: The Root of Overthinking:

At the heart of overthinking lies a deep-seated fear of failure. This fear, universal and potent, acts as a formidable barrier to action and decision-making. It's a fear that whispers tales of caution, urging us to tread lightly lest we stumble and fall. But what fuels this fear, and how does it manifest in the maze of our thoughts?

- Understanding the Fear of Failure

The fear of failure is more than just a fleeting worry; it's a visceral response to the possibility of not meeting our own expectations or those of others. It's rooted in our innate desire for acceptance and belonging and the mistaken belief that our worth is tied to our successes and failures. This fear is magnified in a world that often celebrates victories and glosses over the lessons of defeat, creating a skewed perception of what it means to fail.

- How Fear of Failure Triggers Overthinking

When the fear of failure takes hold, it sets off a cascade of mental simulations. Our minds become battlegrounds where every decision is scrutinised, and every potential outcome is weighed with painstaking detail. We find ourselves trapped in an endless loop of 'what ifs,' paralysed by the prospect of making the wrong choice. This overanalysis is the mind's attempt to shield us from the perceived dangers of failure, but in doing so, it also holds us back from the growth and opportunities that come with taking risks.

- The Consequences of Fear-Driven Overthinking

The impact of this fear-driven overthinking is profound. It stifles creativity, as the fear of judgement silences our inner voice and curbs our willingness to explore new ideas. It hampers decision-making, turning simple choices into Herculean tasks. And perhaps most damagingly, it prevents us from stepping into the arena of action, where the real magic of life unfolds. We miss out on the richness of experience and the lessons of resilience that come from facing our fears head-on.

- Moving Beyond Fear

To transcend the fear of failure, we must first recognise it for what it is: a natural part of the human experience, not a reflection of our worth. By embracing failure as an invaluable teacher and a stepping stone to success, we can begin to shift our perspective. It's about learning to see each misstep not as a mark of defeat but as a catalyst for growth, a chance to refine our strategies and deepen our understanding.

Cultivating a mindset of curiosity and resilience is key. When we approach life with a learner's mindset, every outcome—be it success or failure—becomes a source of insight and strength. This shift doesn't happen overnight, but with practice, we can learn to quiet the fear of failure and channel our mental energy into constructive, empowering action.

2. Desire for Perfection: Why It Can Make Us Overthink:

Trying really hard to be perfect sounds like a good thing, right? But when we always try to make everything perfect, it can actually make us think too much and start doubting ourselves. Here's why:

- Why We Try to Be Perfect

Most of us want to do really well so that others will like and respect us. We think that if we can do everything perfectly, we'll be more successful and happier. This makes us look at every little detail, trying to make sure everything is just right.

- What Happens When We Overthink

But when we try to make everything perfect, we end up thinking too much about it. We worry a lot about making mistakes, and this worry can stop us from doing anything at all. It's like being stuck because we're too afraid of not being perfect. And while we're stuck overthinking, we miss out on fun opportunities and chances to learn from trying and sometimes not getting it right.

- Getting Out of the Perfect Trap

So, how do we stop worrying about being perfect? First, we need to understand that it's okay not to be perfect. Making mistakes is part of learning and getting better at things.

Being kind to ourselves is really important, too. We should treat ourselves the way we'd treat a good friend, understanding that it's okay to mess up sometimes.

Also, making a plan with steps that we can actually do helps us focus on getting things done instead of worrying about making them perfect. Celebrating the small wins along the way makes us feel good and keeps us going.

- Learning to Love Being "Not Perfect"

In the end, it's not about lowering our goals but realising that it's okay not to be perfect. This doesn't mean we stop trying to do well; it just means we understand that messing up sometimes is part of the deal. And that's okay. It's through these little mess-ups that we learn the most and become stronger.

So, let's not worry too much about being perfect. Let's just do our best, learn as we go, and enjoy the journey. This way, we free ourselves from overthinking and start having more fun and success along the way.

3. Lack of Confidence: How It Leads to Overthinking

When we're not feeling confident, we often start thinking too much. This happens because we're worried we're not good enough or that we can't do things right. It's like our brain is trying to solve a puzzle about how we can avoid making mistakes or looking bad.

- Why Feeling Not Confident Makes Us Think Too Much

Feeling unsure about ourselves is pretty normal, but it can make our minds go into overdrive. We start thinking about all the things that could go wrong or questioning if we're doing things right. It's like our mind is working overtime to make up for feeling like we're not enough.

- The Problem with Thinking Too Much Because of Low Confidence

The tricky part is that the more we think to try to avoid mistakes, the more we end up doubting ourselves. It's a cycle that keeps going around – we think too much, then we feel even less confident, and then we think even more. Instead of helping, all this thinking just makes us feel stuck and unsure.

- How to Feel More Confident and Think Less

To break out of overthinking because we're not feeling confident, we need to start focusing on what we're good at. Everyone has things they're good at or times when they've done well. Remembering these can help us feel better about ourselves.

Making small goals and achieving them can also help us feel more confident. It's like proving to ourselves that we can do things well. Being around people who support us and make us feel good is important, too – they remind us of our strengths when we forget.

It's also okay not to be perfect at everything. Learning to be okay with making mistakes is part of getting more confident. It's about being real with ourselves, knowing we're trying our best and that it's okay to learn as we go.

- In Simple Words

Building confidence helps us not to overthink. It's about changing how we see ourselves, focusing on our strengths, and being okay with not being perfect. As we get more confident, we'll find we don't need to think too much about everything. We'll start to trust ourselves more, make decisions easier, and enjoy life more because we're not stuck in our heads all the time. Let's try to be kind to ourselves, take small steps, and remember that it's okay to grow and learn every day.

4. Overwhelm from Information Overload: Navigating the Flood of Data

In our modern, hyper-connected world, we're bombarded with more information in a day than our ancestors might have encountered in a year. This constant stream of data, from news updates to social media feeds, can be overwhelming, especially for those prone to overthinking. Trying to sort through so much information can make our brains freeze up and stop us from thinking clearly, where making decisions becomes as challenging as navigating a ship through a stormy sea.

- Understanding Information Overload

Information overload occurs when we're exposed to more information than our brains can comfortably handle. It's like trying to drink water from a fire hose—instead of quenching our thirst, we end up drenched and overwhelmed. For overthinkers, this excess of data triggers a cascade of analysis as they attempt to process, evaluate, and make sense of every piece of information they encounter.

This relentless pursuit of understanding and the fear of missing out on important details can cause a mental logjam. The mind becomes cluttered with thoughts, ideas, and possibilities, making it difficult to focus on the task at hand or to make decisions. The irony is palpable; in our quest to stay informed and make the best choices, we often find ourselves paralysed, unable to move forward.

- The Impact of Information Overload on Overthinkers

For those inclined to overthink, information overload exacerbates their tendency to dwell on decisions. They might find themselves stuck in a loop of analysis, weighing the pros and cons of each option ad infinitum. This can lead to decision fatigue, where even the simplest choices become daunting tasks. The constant second-guessing drains energy and undermines confidence, leaving individuals feeling stuck and frustrated.

Moreover, the stress associated with information overload can have tangible effects on well-being. The pressure to stay up-to-date and make informed decisions can lead to anxiety, sleep disturbances, and a general sense of dissatisfaction. It's a cycle that feeds into itself; the more overwhelmed we feel, the more we overthink, and the more we overthink, the more overwhelmed we become.

- Strategies to Navigate Information Overload

Breaking free from the grip of information overload requires intentional strategies to manage the flow of data and our reaction to it. Here are some steps to regain control:

1. Set Information Boundaries: Establish limits on how much time you spend consuming information. Be selective about your sources and focus on quality over quantity.

2. Practice Mindful Consumption: Approach information with mindfulness, staying present and engaged rather than passively scrolling through endless feeds.

3. Prioritise and Organise: Determine what information is truly relevant and necessary. Use tools and techniques to organise data in a way that makes it manageable and accessible.

4. Take Breaks: Regularly stepping away from information sources can help clear your mind and reduce the pressure to process everything at once.

5. Trust Your Instincts: Remember that not every decision requires exhaustive research. Sometimes, it's okay to rely on your intuition.

- Embracing a Balanced Approach

Let us then approach the vast sea of information not as a force to be conquered but as a resource to be navigated with care and intention. In doing so, we empower ourselves to move through the world with confidence, making informed decisions without succumbing to the paralysis of overthinking.

5. Lack of Clarity in Goals:

Unclear goals can contribute to overthinking.

Having clear goals is like having a map for a big adventure. It shows us where we want to go and helps us make decisions about how to get there. But when our goals aren't clear, it's easy to feel lost and spend too much time thinking about what to do.

- The Power of Crystal-Clear Goals

The importance of having clear, sharply defined goals cannot be overstated. They are the architects of our future, shaping our actions, decisions, and the very contours of our lives. When our goals are clear, every decision becomes imbued with purpose, every action a step forward in the dance of progress. There is a strength in this clarity, a force that propels us forward, cutting through the mire of overthinking with the sharp blade of decisive action.

- Getting Past Overthinking with Clear Goals

To stop overthinking and start doing, we need to make our goals as clear as possible. This means thinking hard about what we really want to achieve and why it matters to us. Once we have a good idea of our destination, deciding how to get there becomes much simpler.

Having clear goals helps us move from thinking to doing. Each choice we make is a step towards reaching our goals, which makes us feel confident and focused. Even when things get tough, knowing our goals can help us keep going.

- Moving Forward with Purpose

Remember, it's okay if the path isn't always smooth. What's important is to keep moving towards our goals, learning and growing along the way. Clear goals are the tools that help us cut through the confusion and take action toward the life we want.

So, let's make our goals clear and start moving toward them. This way, we'll spend less time worrying about what to do next and more time enjoying the journey towards our dreams.

6. Past Traumas and Overthinking: How They're Connected:

Sometimes, the reason we think too much is because of tough or scary things that happened to us before. These bad experiences can stick in our minds and make us worry a lot. We might keep thinking about these past events, trying to figure them out, or worrying they might happen again, which can make us feel really anxious.

- Why Thinking About the Past Makes Us Worry More

When something bad happens, it can leave a mark on how we think and feel. Our brain tries to protect us by remembering these events so we can try to avoid getting hurt again. But this can backfire, making us see danger everywhere and overthink things. We get stuck going over and over old memories, which can make it hard to decide anything or move on.

- How to Feel Better and Stop Overthinking

To start feeling better, we need to understand that our overthinking is our brain's way of trying to protect us. Recognising this can help us start to heal. Here are some ways to help stop the cycle of worrying about the past:

- **Talking to Someone:** It can really help to talk about our feelings with a friend, family member, or a counsellor who can help us work through our memories.

- **Staying in the Present:** Practices like mindfulness can help us focus on what's happening right now instead of getting lost in past events.

- **Questioning Our Thoughts:** Learning to notice when we're stuck in negative thinking patterns and gently reminding ourselves that we don't have to believe everything we think.

- **Finding People Who Get It:** Spending time with friends or groups who understand what we're going through can make us feel less alone and more supported.

Moving Forward:

Healing from past hurts and stopping overthinking isn't quick or easy, but it's really important for living a happier life. It's about giving ourselves a chance to heal from those old wounds and learning to worry less. With time and effort, we can start to let go of these past traumas and enjoy the present more.

"The key to overcoming overthinking lies in cultivating self-confidence, setting clear goals, and taking decisive action. By addressing the root causes, individuals can break free from the overthinking cycle and move towards a more focused and purposeful life."

CHAPTER 3

Symptoms of Overthinking

Let's talk about a common challenge many of us face – overthinking.

Picture this: your mind is like a busy highway, with thoughts racing in all directions. Now, overthinking isn't just a mental game; it also shows up in your physical well-being. Let's break it down:

1. Constant Worrying:

Overthinking is like being stuck on a treadmill in your mind. This treadmill makes you worry about problems over and over, but you don't go anywhere or solve anything. It's like your brain is always on alert, trying to figure out what could go wrong, which makes you feel stuck and scared to do anything.

When you overthink, you keep asking "what if" questions, like "What if something goes wrong?" These questions can make you worry more and stop you from making decisions or acting because you're always thinking about the bad things that could happen.

This constant worrying isn't just bad for your mind; it can also make your body feel bad. You might have trouble sleeping, get headaches, or feel stressed all the time. Overthinking can make you feel down and stop you from doing things that could help you.

2. Difficulty in Decision-Making:

Overthinking is when people think too much about their choices, trying to guess every possible thing that could happen. They want to make the perfect choice so badly that they end up stuck, unable to decide anything. It's like standing at a fork in the road and trying to predict everything that will happen on each path before choosing one. But this just leads to stress and missing out on good chances that come their way.

The problem is overthinkers believe they can avoid mistakes if they think hard enough. But it's impossible to predict everything. Life is full of surprises, and we can't control everything.

If you overthink, you might miss out on fun and opportunities because you're too busy worrying about what could go wrong. This can make you feel even more stressed and stuck. Overthinkers can struggle to make decisions, getting trapped in analysing every detail.

3. Insomnia or Sleep Issues:

An overactive mind can lead to difficulty falling asleep or staying asleep.

When it gets quiet at night, people who think too much find their minds getting even busier. Instead of sleeping, they start worrying about all sorts of things, which makes it hard to fall asleep or stay asleep. This happens because night-time is often the first chance they get to really think about their day and everything they're worried about without any distractions.

Sleep is important for your health, just like eating right and exercising. If you don't sleep well, it can affect your whole life, including how you feel during the day and how well you can do things.

If you're having trouble sleeping because of too many thoughts, remember it's possible to learn how to calm your mind. By practicing and making some changes, you can make your nights more about resting and less about thinking. This way, you can wake up feeling refreshed and ready for the day.

4. Physical Tension:

Overthinking can result in physical tension, leading to headaches or muscle aches. When you think too much about problems and worries, it doesn't just make you feel stressed out in your mind; it can also make your body feel bad. This stress can show up as headaches, muscle pains, and other aches in your body. It's like your body is trying to tell you it's tired of all the worrying.

Think of your body as a mirror that shows what's happening in your mind. If your mind is full of worries, your body reacts by tensing up, as if it's getting ready to deal with a problem. This can make your muscles feel tight and sore, especially around your neck and shoulders, and can give you headaches.

But here's some good news: just as your mind can make your body feel tense, doing things to relax your body can also make your mind feel calmer. Activities like exercising, doing yoga, or just taking deep breaths can help your body relax. When your body feels more relaxed, your mind often does too.

This means taking care of your body is a good way to help take care of your mind. When you make your body feel better by moving and relaxing, it can help stop your mind from overthinking and making you feel stressed. It's all about helping both your mind and body work together to feel good. So, if you're feeling tense from too much thinking, try to move a bit or take a few deep breaths. It can really help make both your body and mind feel better.

5. Repetitive Thoughts:

Overthinkers often grapple with persistent and intrusive thoughts that keep replaying. For people who think too much, their minds are like being stuck in a loop. They keep thinking about the same things over and over, which can make them feel stressed and stuck. It's like their brain won't stop worrying about things that might go wrong or things they wish they could change.

Think of your mind as a garden. For people who overthink, it's like this garden is always in a storm, with the same thoughts spinning around like a tornado. These thoughts are hard to control and can make it tough to feel calm or happy.

To deal with these repeating thoughts, it's important to focus on what's happening right now, in the present moment, instead of getting lost in your worries.

Remember, your thoughts are just a part of you; they don't define who you are.

6. Negative Self-Talk:

Overthinking is often accompanied by a critical inner voice, eroding self-confidence. When you think too much, you might also have a voice in your head that is always criticising you. This voice can make you feel like you're not good enough, no matter what you do. It's like having a bully inside your mind that keeps putting you down, making it hard to feel confident about yourself.

Imagine your mind is like a big, beautiful place where you can create and do amazing things. But, if there's a bully there, it can make everything seem dark and full of doubt. This critical voice is like that bully, telling you negative things and stopping you from feeling good about yourself. It takes away at the beauty of your potential, leaving behind a landscape of 'what ifs' and 'not good enough.' It transforms the mind from a sanctuary of creativity and strength into a prison of self-doubt.

7. Difficulty Concentrating:

Overactive thoughts can hinder concentration and productivity; having too many thoughts all at once can be a problem because it makes it hard to focus and get things done.

Imagine your thoughts are like wild horses. If they run all over the place, they're hard to control. But if you learn to guide them and point them in one direction, you can use their power to help you move faster toward what you want.

The first step to dealing with too many thoughts is to be very clear about what you want. When you know exactly what your goal is, it's easier to ignore the thoughts that don't help you get there.

8. Social Withdrawal:

Overthinking can lead to social anxiety, causing individuals to avoid interactions.

Overthinking means thinking too much about things, especially about social situations, which can make people feel nervous and worried about being around others. People might fear being judged or messing up in some way. This worry can get so bad that it makes them feel physically sick, like having a fast heartbeat or sweating a lot.

Because of this fear, some people start avoiding hanging out with others or going to social events. They think that by not going, they can avoid feeling anxious. But this makes things worse over time. The more they avoid social situations, the scarier these situations seem.

This cycle of overthinking and social anxiety can significantly impact an individual's quality of life. Opportunities for friendship, love, career advancement, and personal growth are lost, not because they are unattainable but because the fear of negative evaluation and the habit of overthinking create a barrier too high to cross.

Recognising these symptoms is the first step toward overcoming overthinking. Let's involve practical strategies, like mindfulness, positive affirmations, and a focus on solutions rather than problems. By implementing these techniques, individuals can break free from the overthinking cycle and lead more productive and fulfilling lives.

CHAPTER 4

How to Overcome Overthinking

Overcoming overthinking involves strategies that help you break the cycle of excessive analysis and worry. As our body needs physical exercise to get fit and healthy, in the same way, our mind also needs some techniques to get fit and healthy.

1. **Practice Mindfulness:** Engage in mindfulness practices such as meditation or focused breathing exercises. These techniques help bring your attention back to the present moment.

2. **Practice Gratitude:** Focus on things you are grateful for in your life. This can shift your perspective from what could go wrong to appreciating what is going right.

3. **Challenge Your Thoughts:** When you catch yourself overthinking, challenge the validity of your thoughts. Ask yourself, "Is this thought based on facts or my assumptions?" This can help you see the situation more clearly.

4. **Schedule Worry Time:** Allocate a specific time in the day to process your worries. Outside this time, if you find yourself overthinking, remind yourself to save it for your "worry time." A maximum of half an hour at the same time every day, allowing the rest of the day to be free from overthinking.

5. **Engage in Physical Activity:** Any kind of physical exercise, such as yoga, swimming, or walking, can help clear your mind, reduce stress, and shift your focus away from overthinking.

6. **Limit Information Intake:** Too much information can fuel overthinking. Try to limit your research or information-gathering to what's truly necessary.

7. **Break Tasks into Smaller Steps:** If overthinking is preventing you from starting a task, break it down into smaller, manageable steps and focus on one step at a time.

   Believe in the power of concentration.

8. **Seek Professional Help:** If overthinking is significantly impacting your life, consider seeking help from a mental health professional who can provide tailored strategies and support.

Procrastination

"Live as if you were to die tomorrow.
Learn as if you were to live forever."

– Mahatma Gandhi

Current Scenario of Procrastination

The Waiting Game: Procrastination and Its Impact

In today's fast-paced, interconnected world, procrastination emerges not merely as a personal challenge but as a global phenomenon affecting millions of professionals across industries. The advent of digital technology, while offering unprecedented opportunities for efficiency and connectivity, has also introduced distractions that can lead to procrastination on a scale never seen before.

The current scenario of procrastination worldwide is marked by a paradox: even as we possess the tools that could enhance our productivity to remarkable levels, the temptation to defer tasks has become more prevalent. Social media, instant messaging, emails, and the vast expanse of the internet present a constant barrage of distractions that can derail even the most disciplined among us.

Yet, it is precisely within this challenge that we find the seeds of opportunity. As I often emphasise, the key to overcoming procrastination lies in understanding its root causes and adopting a strategic approach to managing our time and energy. The global nature of procrastination today calls for a renewed focus on self-discipline, goal setting, and prioritisation—principles that have stood the test of time.

In confronting procrastination, we must first acknowledge it as a natural human tendency rather than a personal failure. This realisation opens the door to strategies designed to counteract procrastination's pull. Techniques such as setting clear, achievable goals (the SMART criteria: Specific, Measurable, Achievable, Relevant, and Time-bound), prioritising tasks using the Eisenhower Matrix, and employing the Pomodoro Technique for time management can transform our approach to work and productivity.

Moreover, the global context in which we find ourselves today highlights the importance of cultivating resilience and adaptability. The rapid pace of change in our professional and personal lives demands a mindset that views challenges, including procrastination, as opportunities for growth and learning. By embracing lifelong learning and remaining open to new experiences and perspectives, we can stay ahead of the curve and maintain our productivity amidst distractions.

To navigate the current scenario of procrastination, it is also crucial to leverage technology judiciously. While digital tools can be sources of distraction, when used effectively, they can enhance our ability to organise, prioritise, and execute tasks. From productivity apps that block distracting websites to software that helps manage tasks and deadlines, technology, when harnessed correctly, can be a powerful ally in our fight against procrastination.

In conclusion, the current global scenario of procrastination challenges us to be more disciplined, focused, and intentional in how we manage our time and energy. By understanding the underlying causes of procrastination and applying proven strategies to overcome it, we can achieve our goals and realise our full potential. The journey toward peak productivity is both a personal and collective endeavour, requiring us to adapt, learn, and grow in an ever-changing world. As we face this challenge head-on, we not only improve our own lives but also contribute to a more productive, efficient, and fulfilling global community.

CHAPTER 2

What is Procrastination?

Time's Thief

The Story of Emma: From Procrastination to Empowerment

Emma was someone you might know. In fact, she could be any one of us. She was ambitious, filled with dreams and aspirations that could light up the night sky. Yet, Emma was also intimately familiar with an invisible force that seemed to hold her back: Procrastination.

Day after day, Emma promised herself she'd start working on her dream project "tomorrow." She wanted to launch her own online business, a venture that combined her passion for wellness with her knack for digital marketing. But every morning, she woke up to the same routine, the same excuses, telling herself she wasn't ready, that she needed more time to research, more time to prepare.

Months slipped into years, and Emma's dream remained just that—a dream. Deep down, she knew procrastination was the culprit, the thief stealing her potential. It wasn't until she attended a seminar, one that promised to ignite change and propel attendees toward their goals, that Emma's story took a dramatic turn.

The speaker was electrifying, his words a mirror reflecting Emma's own internal battles. He spoke of procrastination not as a mere inconvenience but as a critical barrier to living a life of fulfilment and purpose. He described it as a monster, fed by fear and comfort, that grows stronger with every opportunity we let slip through our fingers.

But then, he shared something else, a weapon powerful enough to conquer this monster: the power of decision. The moment we decide to take action, he declared, is the moment we reclaim control over our destiny.

Emma left the seminar transformed. She realised that waiting for the perfect moment was a fool's task. The perfect moment is now. She started small, dedicating just one hour each morning to her project. It was challenging at first, facing the fear of inadequacy and the uncertainty of the unknown. Yet, with each passing day, her confidence grew, and the grip of procrastination loosened.

Six months later, Emma launched her wellness platform. It wasn't perfect, but it was a start—a beautiful, imperfect start. Her website became a beacon for those seeking to improve their lives, and with time, it grew into a thriving community.

Emma's journey from procrastination to empowerment wasn't easy, but it was worth every step. She learned that action is the antidote to fear and that progress, no matter how small, is progress nonetheless. She discovered that the only real failure lies in not starting at all and that each moment is an opportunity to move closer to her dreams.

Towards our goals. Emma's tale is a testimony to the transformative power of action and the potential within each of us to overcome the barriers that hold us back.

Procrastination is not just a habit or a minor personal flaw; it is a significant barrier to unlocking one's full potential.

Procrastination is the thief of time, yes, but more than that, it's the thief of opportunity, of potential, of the very life you dream of living. It's that voice in your head that says, "Tomorrow," when your heart knows the truth should be "Today." It's the invisible chain that holds you back from stepping into your power and living at your peak.

At its core, procrastination is a form of self-sabotage. It's the manifestation of our fears, doubts, and uncertainties. It whispers lies of comfort in the form of waiting for the 'perfect' moment, which, in reality, never comes. Every moment spent in the grasp of procrastination is a moment when we're not living our true purpose, not chasing our dreams, and not contributing our unique gifts to the world.

But here's the kicker: Procrastination is not about laziness. No, it's much deeper than that. It's about fear. Fear of failure, fear of success, fear of stepping out of our comfort zones. It's about the stories we tell ourselves about who we are, what we're capable of, and what we deserve. And these stories, these limiting beliefs, they're the fuel for the fire of procrastination.

However, this is where the magic happens: the moment we decide to confront these fears to change our story, that's the moment we break free. Procrastination can be overcome, not by sheer willpower alone, but by transforming our mindset, setting compelling goals that ignite our passion, and taking massive, determined action towards achieving them.

It's about redefining our relationship with discomfort, embracing it as a necessary companion on the journey to growth and achievement. Every step taken in action is a step away from the shadow of procrastination and into the light of potential realised.

Remember, in the grand scheme of your life, the actions you take today shape your tomorrow. The power to change, to move beyond procrastination, lies within you, in the decisions you make right now. It's about deciding that your dreams are bigger than your fears and that your goals are too important to be left for 'someday.' It's about creating a life of 'no regrets,' where you've lived fully, loved deeply, and contributed meaningfully.

So, let's not give procrastination the power to dictate our lives. Let's reclaim our power, our agency. Let's commit to action, to living boldly and with purpose. Because in the end, the only thing standing between you and your dreams is the action you haven't yet taken. Let's take that step together now.

CHAPTER 3

Science Behind Procrastination

Harnessing Biology to Beat Procrastination

In the energising and insightful tone, the biology of procrastination is explored not just as a mere habit but as a deeply ingrained part of our neurological and psychological makeup. Let's delve deep into the science behind procrastination.

As we embark on the journey to understand and conquer procrastination, it's crucial to peel back the layers and explore the very fabric of our being—our biology. Yes, my friends, procrastination isn't just a bad habit; it's woven into our neurological and psychological architecture. But here's the empowering truth: by understanding the biology of procrastination, we can rewire our brains and reclaim our power to act, achieve, and thrive.

At the heart of procrastination lies the battle between two parts of the brain: the prefrontal cortex, the region associated with planning and decision-making, and the limbic system, one of the oldest and most dominant portions of the brain, which is responsible for our emotional responses, including pleasure. When we procrastinate, it's often because the limbic system is winning the battle over the prefrontal cortex, choosing immediate pleasure or the avoidance of discomfort over long-term goals and rewards.

This biological tug-of-war is further complicated by the release of dopamine, a neurotransmitter associated with feelings of pleasure and reward. When we choose a pleasurable activity over a challenging task, our brain rewards us with a dopamine hit, reinforcing the procrastination behaviour. It's a cycle that can be tough to break but not impossible.

Now, let's talk about stress. Chronic stress triggers the release of cortisol, which can impair cognitive functions and make us more likely to seek comfort in procrastination. It's our body's way of saying, "This is too much; let's take a break and do something less taxing." While this might have been helpful in our evolutionary past, in the modern world, it often leads us away from our goals.

But here's where it gets exciting: we have the power to rewire our brains. Neuroplasticity, the brain's ability to form new neural connections throughout life, means that we can train our brain to favour productive behaviour over procrastination. By creating new habits, setting clear and compelling goals, and taking consistent action, we can strengthen the neural pathways that support focus, discipline, and achievement.

Imagine conditioning your brain to crave the fulfilment of completing tasks rather than the temporary pleasure of putting them off. It's about shifting your focus from immediate gratification to the long-term satisfaction and joy that come from living a life aligned with your deepest values and aspirations.

So, how do we leverage this knowledge to beat procrastination? It starts with awareness. Recognise when you're about to procrastinate and pause to consider the biological forces at play. Then, engage your prefrontal cortex by reminding yourself of your larger goals and the reasons they matter to you. Break tasks into smaller, manageable steps to reduce the emotional resistance from your limbic system. And celebrate your wins, however small, to create positive dopamine associations with productivity.

In embracing the biology of procrastination, we unlock a powerful ally in our quest for personal growth and achievement. Remember, the ultimate power lies not in our biology but in our ability to understand and direct it toward our highest goals and dreams. Let's harness the incredible machinery of our brain to break free from the chains of procrastination and step into our greatness.

In this example, the knowledge of our biological predispositions can be a powerful tool for change. By understanding why we procrastinate and applying targeted strategies to counteract these tendencies, we can overcome the barriers to our success and achieve our full potential.

The Transformation of Alex:

Alex, a software developer with a passion for creating innovative apps, found himself trapped in the cycle of procrastination. Despite his ambitions, he often ended up scrolling through social media, watching videos, or engaging in any activity other than working on his app development projects. He knew he was procrastinating but couldn't seem to break free from its grip.

After attending a seminar on personal growth, where the biology of procrastination was explained, Alex had an epiphany. He realised that his brain was choosing immediate pleasure over the long-term satisfaction of completing his projects. Armed with this new understanding, Alex decided to implement a plan that leveraged his biology to overcome procrastination.

First, Alex focused on breaking his tasks into smaller, more manageable steps. He understood that his brain was overwhelmed by the magnitude of his projects, triggering stress responses that fuelled his procrastination. By simplifying his tasks, he reduced the emotional resistance from his limbic system, making it easier to start and maintain momentum.

Next, Alex introduced a reward system. Every time he completed a task, he allowed himself a small reward, such as a 10-minute break to enjoy a coffee or a short walk outside. This strategy utilised dopamine to his advantage, reinforcing productive behaviour by associating task completion with pleasure.

Furthermore, Alex began practicing mindfulness and stress-reduction techniques. He recognised that stress was a significant factor in his procrastination habit, impairing his prefrontal cortex's ability to make rational decisions. Through meditation and deep-breathing exercises, he lowered his stress levels, enhancing his focus and decision-making capabilities.

Perhaps most importantly, Alex started visualising his goals daily. Each morning, he spent a few minutes imagining the success of his apps, the impact they would have on users, and the personal satisfaction he would feel. This visualisation technique engaged his prefrontal cortex, strengthening his internal motivation and resilience against procrastination.

Over time, Alex noticed a profound shift in his behaviour. Tasks that once seemed daunting now felt achievable. He found joy in the process of creation, and the cycle of procrastination that had hindered his progress began to dissolve. His projects moved forward, and he released his first app to critical acclaim.

Alex's story is a testament to the power of understanding and leveraging our biology to overcome procrastination. By breaking tasks into smaller steps, rewarding himself for progress, managing stress, and visualising success, Alex transformed his approach to work and life. His journey illustrates that with the right strategies, it's possible to rewire our brains for productivity and fulfilment, turning our dreams into reality.

CHAPTER 4

Types of Procrastination

In this chapter dedicated to unravelling the complexities of procrastination, I, with my characteristic blend of enthusiasm and depth, would dive into the different types of procrastination that people face. My approach would not only classify these types but also offer insights into overcoming each, turning understanding into a springboard for action.

The Many Faces of Procrastination (types):

Welcome to a journey into the heart of procrastination, a phenomenon that's as multifaceted as it is misunderstood. You see, procrastination isn't just a singular entity; it's a shapeshifter, manifesting in various forms depending on our fears, motivations, and life circumstances. Recognising which type of procrastination holds sway over you is the first step in reclaiming your power and steering your life toward your dreams.

1. The Perfectionist Procrastinator

The perfectionist procrastinator is caught in the trap of wanting everything to be flawless. This type fears making mistakes and often feels that if something can't be done perfectly, it's better not to do it at all. But here's the truth: perfection is an illusion, a mirage in the desert of productivity. The key to overcoming this form of procrastination is to embrace imperfection as a natural part of growth. Set yourself free by setting realistic standards and celebrating progress, not perfection.

2. The Overwhelmed Procrastinator

Feeling overwhelmed is like standing at the base of a mountain, looking up at the peak, and thinking, "I can't possibly climb this." The overwhelmed procrastinator is paralysed by the sheer volume or difficulty of tasks ahead. The antidote? Break the mountain into hills. Divide your tasks into smaller, manageable steps, and focus on completing just one step at a time. With each step, the summit becomes more attainable.

3. The Fearful Procrastinator

Fear of failure, fear of success, fear of the unknown—these are the spectres that haunt the fearful procrastinator. This type avoids starting or completing tasks because of the deep-seated fears of what might (or might not) happen. Confronting your fears is the way forward. Ask yourself, "What's the worst that can happen?" More often than not, you'll realise the fear is far worse than any potential reality. Face your fears head-on and use them as steppingstones rather than stumbling blocks.

4. The "Thrill-Seeker" Procrastinator

For some, the rush of last-minute work is intoxicating. This type of procrastinates deliberately to experience the adrenaline rush of racing against the clock. While this might work on occasion, it's a risky and stressful way to live. To shift away from this habit, start associating pleasure with the peace and satisfaction of completing tasks well ahead of deadlines. Find your thrills in achievement, not in the ticking of the clock.

5. The Indecisive Procrastinator

Decision paralysis can be a profound source of procrastination. The indecisive procrastinator is stuck in limbo, afraid of making the wrong choice. The remedy? Embrace the power of decision-making. Understand that making a decision, even if it's not the perfect one, propels you forward. Learn to trust your intuition, make the best choice you can with the information you have, and adjust your course as you go.

Transforming Understanding into Action:

Identifying your type of procrastination is like shining a light into the shadows; it's the first step toward dispelling the darkness. Each type has its roots in our fears, habits, and beliefs, but with awareness and targeted action, we can overcome them. Remember, the goal isn't to never procrastinate again—that's unrealistic. The goal is to understand why we procrastinate and to manage it in ways that empower us rather than hold us back.

In this chapter, we've explored the landscape of procrastination, but the journey doesn't end here. It's time to take this knowledge and turn it into action. Start by identifying which type of procrastinator you are, then apply the strategies we've discussed. Your dreams deserve the best of you, and the best of you requires action. Let's move forward, not someday, but today.

In this chapter, I would like you to not only recognise and understand your procrastination patterns but also to feel equipped and motivated to confront and overcome them, paving the way for personal growth and achievement.

CHAPTER 5

Unravelling the Roots of Procrastination

From Dreamer to Doer

Welcome to a journey into the heart of procrastination, a place where dreams are deferred, and potential remains untapped. But fear not, for understanding the roots of this pervasive habit is the first step toward liberation. Procrastination isn't a sign of laziness or lack of ambition; it's a complex interplay of psychological factors, emotional challenges, and even biological predispositions. Let's explore these causes and, more importantly, how we can rise above them.

1. The Fear Factor: Turning Fear into Your Fuel for Success:

In the landscape of personal achievement and the pursuit of our goals, there exists a formidable adversary, one that has the power to stop us in our tracks and cloak our dreams in the shadows of hesitation and doubt. This adversary is fear. Fear of failure, fear of success, and fear of venturing beyond the familiar borders of our comfort zones. It manifests as a psychological barrier, an instinctive mechanism designed to protect us, yet often it serves to detain us.

Fear is the root of procrastination. It whispers tales of caution, painting pictures of failure and disappointment or conjuring visions of success that carry the weight of expectation and change.

It's not the desire to avoid success that leads us to procrastinate, but rather the fear of what achieving our dreams might demand of us or alter in our lives.

However, within this very fear lies the seed of transformation. The journey to overcoming fear and, consequently, procrastination is not about denying the existence of fear but about recognising it, embracing it, and then moving through it with deliberate action. Courage, my friends, is the essence of recognising your fear and deciding to take action regardless of it. It's about making the conscious decision that the pursuit of your goals and the realisation of your potential is greater than any fear.

- Acknowledge Your Fear

  The first step in transforming fear into your ally is to acknowledge it. Identify what you're afraid of. Is it the fear of not being good enough? The fear of rejection? Or perhaps the fear of the unknown that success brings? By naming your fear, you strip it of its nebulous power over you, turning it into a challenge that can be addressed and overcome.

- Reframe Your Fear

  Once you've identified your fear, reframe it. See it not as a stop sign but as a signpost guiding you toward areas in your life that are ripe for growth and development. Failure, when reframed, becomes a lesson; success is an opportunity for further expansion and exploration. Ask yourself, "What can I learn from this fear?" Use these insights as steppingstones to build a stronger, more resilient mindset.

- Take Massive Action

  The antidote to fear is action—massive, determined action. Action transforms fear from a paralysing force into a propellant that drives you forward. Start with small steps if you must but start. Each action you take in the face of fear reinforces your courage, builds your confidence, and diminishes the power fear holds over you. Remember, motion creates emotion. The more you move toward your fears, the less intimidating they become, and the more you fuel your growth and progress.

- Leverage Fear as a Motivator

Instead of allowing fear to be a barrier, use it as a motivator. Let the energy of fear propel you forward, transforming it into excitement and anticipation for what lies ahead. Every great achievement involves navigating through fears and uncertainties. It's in these moments of challenge that we discover our true strength and potential.

- Celebrate Your Courage

Finally, celebrate your courage. Each time you take action despite your fear, you're not only moving closer to your goals but also building a stronger, more fearless version of yourself. Acknowledge these victories, no matter how small, and let them serve as reminders of your capability to overcome obstacles and chase your dreams.

2. Overwhelm and Decision Paralysis: The Pathway to Clarity and Action:

Feeling overwhelmed by the sheer volume or complexity of tasks can lead to procrastination. In the grand tapestry of our lives, where ambitions are vast and the hours in a day are limited, it's all too easy to find ourselves at the mercy of overwhelm. This sensation, akin to standing at the centre of a whirlwind of tasks, each clamouring for attention, can immobilise even the most determined among us. Decision paralysis sets in, a fog that clouds our judgement, making every choice seem insurmountable. Yet, it is within this very whirlwind that opportunity lies—a chance to rise, to clarify our intentions, and to move forward with unwavering purpose.

- Embrace the Power of Clarity

The first step in cutting through the noise is to seek clarity. Clarity is not just about knowing what needs to be done; it's about understanding why it matters. Begin by asking yourself, "What are my ultimate goals? What are the tasks that truly align with my vision for my life?" These questions will serve as a lighthouse, guiding you through the storm of tasks and distractions, illuminating the path that leads toward your true objectives.

- The Art of Prioritisation

With clarity comes the ability to prioritise. Not all tasks are created equal, and recognising this is crucial. The power of prioritisation means focusing our energy where it counts the most. Use tools like the Pareto Principle or the 80/20 rule, which posits that 80% of our results come from 20% of our efforts. Identify those tasks that yield the highest impact and allocate your resources accordingly. This is not just about doing more; it's about doing more of what matters.

- Break Down the Giants

Overwhelm thrives on complexity and volume. The antidote? Break down your tasks into smaller, manageable steps. The power of breaking down seemingly insurmountable tasks into bite-sized actions. Each small step taken is a victory against paralysis, a move toward momentum. Remember, progress is cumulative; every small action adds up, building a foundation of achievement that can withstand the pressures of overwhelm.

- Decision-Making as a Skill

  Decision paralysis often stems from a fear of making the wrong choice. Decision-making is a skill honed through practice and resilience. Make decisions swiftly, learn from the outcomes, and adjust your course as needed. Embrace the philosophy that there are no failures, only outcomes. Each decision, whether it leads to success or provides a valuable lesson, is a step forward.

- Cultivate a Mindset of Action

  Finally, The importance of cultivating a mindset of action. Overwhelm and decision paralysis lose their grip when confronted with decisive action. Action breeds clarity, and clarity breeds more action. It's a virtuous cycle, one that propels us from the sidelines of our lives into the arena where our dreams and aspirations are fought for and realised.

3. The Lure of Instant Gratification:

In today's fast-paced society, the siren call of instant gratification is louder and more enticing than ever before. We find ourselves immersed in a culture that admires the immediate, the now, the effortlessly attainable. Whether it's the quick dopamine hit from a social media notification, the rush of an online purchase, or the comfort of binge-watching a series, the temptation to prioritise immediate pleasure over enduring fulfilment is a pervasive challenge.

This quest for instant satisfaction, while seemingly benign at the moment, can tangle us in a cycle of procrastination and short-sighted decision-making. It's a seductive trap that whispers promises of comfort and ease yet often leads us away from our true aspirations and potential. The tasks and goals that truly matter—the ones that require perseverance, effort, and time—do not typically offer the quick rewards our brains have been conditioned to seek. And so, we delay, we divert, and we distract ourselves from the path of meaningful achievement.

Yet, it is within our power to resist this charm, recalibrate our focus, and realign our actions with our deeper, more significant objectives. Cultivating discipline is not merely a matter of willpower; it's an act of profound self-love and respect. It's a commitment to our future selves, an investment in our dreams and our well-being.

To navigate beyond the enticing maze of instant gratification, we must anchor ourselves to our long-term vision. This requires clarity about what we truly want, why it matters, and how each step we take brings us closer to our ultimate goals. It's about creating a compelling future that pulls us forward and makes the immediate sacrifices and efforts worthwhile.

Imagine your life as a grand tapestry, each thread representing a choice, an action, a moment. The threads of instant gratification may add bright, fleeting colours, but it's the deeper, more substantial strands that give the tapestry its richness and beauty. These are the threads woven from discipline, perseverance, and the pursuit of meaningful goals. They are what transform a simple fabric into a masterpiece.

As we stand at the crossroads of now versus later, let us choose the path that leads to lasting fulfilment. Let's embrace the discipline required to transcend the lure of the immediate to build a life of purpose, achievement, and true happiness. It's a journey that demands courage, commitment, and an unwavering focus on our deeper values and aspirations.

Remember, the choice to pursue long-term success over instant gratification is a declaration of faith in ourselves and our dreams. It's a choice that shapes not only our future but the very essence of who we are becoming. Let us make that choice with conviction, embracing the challenges and the rewards that come with living a life aligned with our highest potential.

4. Perfectionism: The Good and The Bad:

Imagine you're playing a video game where you want to get the highest score ever. You try so hard to be perfect that you're scared to make even a tiny mistake. This is what being a perfectionist is like. You want to do everything so well that sometimes you might not even start because you're afraid you won't be perfect.

Perfectionism is like a coin with two sides. One side makes you want to do amazing things and reach for really high goals. This sounds good because it can help you do your best work, like creating awesome projects or coming up with cool ideas. But the other side of the coin can make you feel stuck. You might worry so much about not being perfect that you don't try new things or finish your homework because you're scared it won't be perfect.

But here's a secret: making mistakes is okay! Actually, it's more than okay. When we mess up, we learn from it, and it helps us get better. Think about it like playing a new level in a game. The first few times, you might not do so well, but each time you play, you learn more about how to beat it. Making mistakes and not being perfect all the time is how we learn and grow.

So, instead of always trying to be perfect, we can try to just get better bit by bit. This means being okay with not getting everything right the first time and knowing that it's part of learning. We can try new things, learn from what goes wrong, and keep getting better.

Being perfect isn't the goal; getting better and learning is. All the great things people have done didn't happen because they were perfect from the start. They happened because people weren't afraid to try, make mistakes, and keep improving.

So, let's not worry about being perfect all the time. Let's be brave and try new things, learn from our mistakes, and know that every step we take, even if it's not perfect, is helping us grow and become even better at what we do. This way, we can all reach for our goals, learn loads, and have fun along the way without being scared of not being perfect.

Lack of Motivation and Unclear Goals: Finding Your Way:

When we don't have clear goals or a strong reason to do something, it's super easy to keep putting things off. Think of it like this: if you don't know where you want to go, how can you get excited about starting the trip? If our goals feel too far away or we're not really sure why they're important to us, we lose the push to take action right now.

But here's how we can fix that: by making sure our goals are really clear and mean something special to us. Goals shouldn't be just random things we think we should do; they should be like dreams that light us up inside, things that make us really want to jump out of bed in the morning.

To find these kinds of goals, we need to ask ourselves some big questions, like what really makes us happy, what we care about the most, and why these things are so important to us. It's all about digging deep and figuring out what we truly want, not what someone else thinks we should want.

Once we know what our goals are, we have to make them super clear in our minds. We should be able to see them, feel them, and almost touch them in our imagination. This makes them feel real and doable, not just like wishes that might never come true.

Getting from being stuck and not motivated to being excited and on the move isn't always easy, but it's definitely worth it. It means really getting to know ourselves, what we love, and what we want to achieve. And when we start working towards goals that mean a lot to us, we find a special kind of energy that comes from inside and keeps us going, even when things get tough.

So, let's make our goals clear and find that inner spark that makes us want to go after them. This is how we get moving, reach our dreams, and live a life that feels full and true to who we are. It's about being our best selves and lighting the way for others, too.

Transforming Insight into Action: The Journey Beyond Procrastination:

Embarking on the journey to understand the roots of procrastination is a commendable first stride toward liberation. Yet, true transformation unfolds when insight catalyses into decisive action. Within each reason for the delay, within every moment of hesitation, lies a golden opportunity for a breakthrough. It is in the confrontation of our fears, the simplification of our tasks into achievable segments, the pursuit of lasting satisfaction over fleeting pleasure, the acceptance of our flaws, and the sharpening of our vision that the chains of procrastination begin to dissolve.

The essence of change does not dwell in the realm of perfection but in the domain of persistence. The journey ahead is not marked by the absence of obstacles but by our resolve to navigate through them. It's a path paved with the bricks of small yet significant steps forward. Each step, no matter its size, is a testament to our resilience, a declaration of our commitment to the life we yearn for and richly deserve.

Let this be our rallying cry: to convert the understanding of procrastination's causes into a series of deliberate actions. Face each fear not as an insurmountable barrier but as a challenge to be met with courage and wisdom. Break down each task not as a means to diminish their importance but to amplify our capacity to engage with them fully. Seek not the instant gratification that fades with the setting sun but the enduring fulfilment that dawns with purpose and passion. Embrace not the illusion of perfection but the beauty of progress, knowing that each imperfection is a brushstroke in the masterpiece of our lives. Clarify our goals with such precision that they beckon us forward, illuminating our path with clarity and conviction.

Remember, the reservoir of power to instigate change resides within each of us. It is a power not bestowed by external validation but kindled by our inner flame. It is not the absence of fear but the presence of courage that defines us. It is not the scale of the step that matters but the decision to take it.

As we stand on the precipice of transformation, let us pledge to move from insight to action, from contemplation to courage, from procrastination to progress. Let us commit, here and now, to take that first step, however small, towards the life we envision. Each step is a victory, a liberation from the inertia that once held us captive, propelling us toward the destiny we desire and deserve.

This is not merely a journey; it is an odyssey of self-discovery, empowerment, and realisation. As we traverse this path, let each step remind us of our strength, our potential, and our capacity to overcome. Let us forge ahead, persistent and undeterred, knowing that the life we aspire to is not just a distant dream but a reality waiting to be realised through our actions.

In this commitment to action, we find not only the antidote to procrastination but the key to unlocking our fullest potential. Let us embrace this journey with open hearts and steadfast determination, for it is in the act of moving forward that we truly find ourselves and the life we seek.

Unveiling the Symptoms of Procrastination: A Guide to Recognition and Empowerment

In the vast landscape of human behaviour, procrastination stands as a silent destroyer of dreams and ambitions. It's a cunning adversary, often cloaked in the guise of 'waiting for the right moment' or 'needing to do more research.' Recognising the symptoms of procrastination is the first critical step toward reclaiming control of our time, energy, and potential. As we peel back the layers of this pervasive issue, we uncover a series of tell-tale signs that signal its presence in our lives.

- **Chronic Delay:** The most evident symptom of procrastination is the consistent postponement of tasks. It's the pattern of telling ourselves we'll start "tomorrow," only for each tomorrow to become another day of delay. This cycle of postponement becomes a barrier to our progress, a perpetual loop that keeps our goals just out of reach.

- **Overwhelming Sense of Dread:** Procrastination is often accompanied by a mounting sense of dread towards the task at hand. This isn't merely a lack of enthusiasm but a profound aversion that grows stronger with each passing day. It's as if the task casts a long shadow over our thoughts, sapping our energy before we've even begun.

- **Rationalisation:** One of the more insidious symptoms of procrastination is our ability to rationalise the delay. We become masters of justification, crafting elaborate reasons why now is not the "ideal" time. These rationalisations serve as a smokescreen, hiding the underlying fear or resistance that holds us back.

- **Busywork Overload:** Engaging in busywork is another classic sign of procrastination. We fill our time with tasks of marginal importance, creating a facade of productivity. This diversion tactic allows us to feel a sense of accomplishment while sidestepping the more significant, challenging tasks that demand our attention.

- **Decline in Performance:** As procrastination takes hold, a noticeable decline in the quality of our work often follows. The rush to meet deadlines compromises our standards, leading to outcomes that fall short of our true capabilities. This erosion of quality can affect not just the task at hand but our overall sense of self-worth and achievement.

- **Increased Stress and Anxiety:** The weight of unfinished tasks and looming deadlines contributes to heightened stress and anxiety levels. This emotional toll is a direct consequence of procrastination, creating a feedback loop where stress fuels further delay, which, in turn, amplifies stress.

- **Avoidance of Decision-Making:** Procrastination can manifest as an avoidance of making decisions, big or small. This hesitation to commit reflects a deeper uncertainty and fear of taking decisive action, effectively paralysing progress.

Recognising these symptoms within ourselves is not an exercise in self-reproach but a call to action. It is an invitation to confront the patterns that hinder our growth and to step into our power. Each symptom, while a challenge, also presents an opportunity for transformation. By acknowledging the presence of procrastination, we arm ourselves with the knowledge and insight needed to transcend it.

The journey beyond procrastination begins with awareness, but it is sustained by the deliberate choices we make each day. Let us choose to face our tasks with courage, embrace the discomfort of growth, and forge a path toward our highest aspirations. In doing so, we not only overcome procrastination but also unlock the full measure of our potential.

Techniques to Overcome Procrastination: Mastering the Art of Action

Procrastination, the silent thief of time, has a way of creeping into our lives, holding us back from achieving our fullest potential. But the power to conquer this foe lies within each of us, ready to be unleashed. Through a series of transformative techniques, we can turn the tide against procrastination and step into a world of productivity, achievement, and fulfilment.

1. **Set Compelling Goals:** Begin by crafting goals that ignite your passion and excite your spirit. These shouldn't be ordinary goals but ones that speak to your deepest desires and aspirations. When your goals stir your emotions, they become magnetic, pulling you forward with an irresistible force.

2. **Break It Down:** Facing a monumental task can be daunting and a common cause for delay. The solution? Break your goals into small, manageable steps. Each step should be clear and achievable, transforming the journey from overwhelming to enjoyable. Celebrate each milestone, reinforcing your path with positive reinforcement.

3. **Embrace the Power of Now:** Procrastination often masquerades as a benign decision to delay action until 'later.' Challenge this notion by embracing the power

of now. Ask yourself, "What's one action I can take immediately?" This shifts your mindset from passivity to action, creating a ripple effect that propels you forward.

4. **Leverage the Five-Second Rule:** When you feel hesitation creeping in, employ the five-second rule. Count down from five to one, and at one, propel yourself into action. This simple technique interrupts the procrastination loop and triggers a mental shift from thinking to doing.

5. **Create an Environment for Success:** Your environment plays a crucial role in your productivity. Design a space that minimises distractions and maximises focus. This might mean decluttering your workspace, using tools that block digital distractions, or setting specific hours dedicated to deep work.

6. **Commit Publicly:** Accountability can be a powerful motivator. Share your goals with someone you trust, or even better, commit publicly. When others are aware of your intentions, the desire to uphold your commitment and avoid letting them down can drive you to action.

7. **Find Your Why:** Understanding the deeper purpose behind your actions provides a wellspring of motivation. When faced with procrastination, revisit your 'why'. Remind yourself of the reasons you embarked on this journey, and let that clarity and purpose guide you through moments of hesitation.

8. **Practice Self-Compassion:** Be kind to yourself. Procrastination is a common challenge, and berating yourself only fuels the cycle of delay. Recognise that every journey has its setbacks, and treat yourself with the same compassion you would offer a friend. This fosters a positive mindset conducive to growth and progress.

9. **Visualise Success:** Harness the power of visualisation by imagining the successful completion of your goals. Feel the satisfaction, the joy, and the pride of achievement. This mental rehearsal primes your subconscious for success, making action feel like the natural next step.

10. **Embrace Imperfection:** Perfectionism is procrastination's close ally. Release the need for everything to be perfect and allow yourself to make progress, however imperfect. Remember, progress, not perfection, is the goal.

By integrating these techniques into your daily life, you embark on a transformative journey from procrastination to productivity. Each strategy is a tool, empowering you to take control of your time, your actions, and, ultimately, your life. Let this be the moment you choose to rise above procrastination, unleash your potential, and create the life you desire and deserve. Together, let's step into action, into achievement, and into a future filled with endless possibilities.

Conclusion

Panic to Power will give you the ability to…

- Control and find your strength, even when things get tough. This book is more than just words on pages – it's a guide to making big changes in your life.

- How to stay strong and calm when you're under a lot of pressure.

- The big goals you've always wanted to achieve but maybe were too scared to try. You'll learn how to bring these dreams to life and make them real.

- Cutting-edge strategies to think smarter, not harder. Setting a new standard for yourself, where 'good enough' becomes 'better than ever before.'

- Tackle the habits that stop you from succeeding. We all sometimes get in our own way, but you'll learn how to stop doing that and move forward instead.

- Building real confidence is also important. Feel good about yourself and be ready to take on any challenge.

- It's about discovering the hero inside you. You already have everything you need to be great – this book will help you see that and use your strengths to overcome any challenge.

This book is about taking action and making changes. It's about growing, becoming more confident, and achieving your goals. Are you ready to start? Let's go on this journey together!

Call to Action

Are You...

- Grappling with stress, overthinking, or procrastination in ways that feel overwhelming or unique to your life situation.

- Applying the strategies in this book, I feel you're skimming the surface of a deeper, more personal issue.

- Eager for personalised advice that goes beyond the scope of this book.

- Looking for someone to talk to who understands the intricacies of these challenges and can offer guidance and help overcome them.

- Looking for a mentor or coach who can provide a more tailored, one-on-one approach to managing your challenges.

Is This You?

Then Nidhi Nair can help you create the future you deserve

www.nidhinair.com

Send us an email at life@nidhinair.com and say: "Let's Talk"

"The world needs more great leaders."